BULL RUN!

THE STORY OF THE 1995-96 CHICAGO BULLS: THE GREATEST TEAM IN BASKETBALL HISTORY

by Roland Lazenby
Foreword by Phil Jackson
Photography by Bill Smith

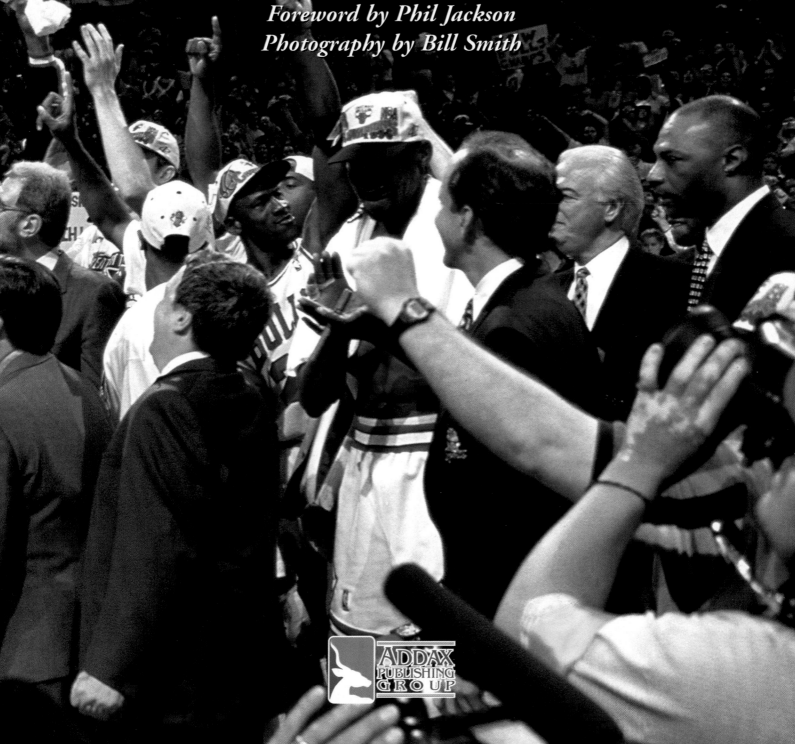

ADDAX
PUBLISHING
GROUP

Author's Acknowledgments

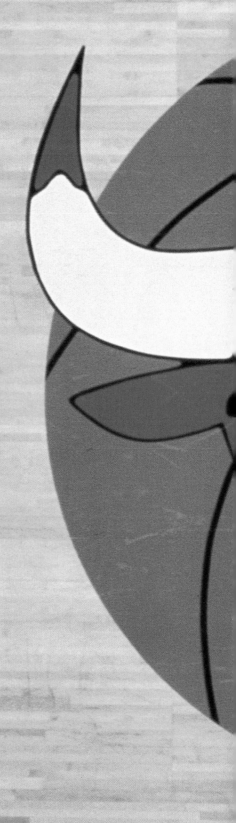

One of the reasons the Bulls are world champions is the first-rate people they have running the show. I want to thank Steve Schanwald, the team's marketing and broadcasting vice president, for his belief in this project. And their media relations team – Tim Hallam, Lori Flores, Tom Smithburg and interns Sarah Graves-Beckley and Larvetta Loftin – is the best. Also the gang at Addax Publishing – publisher Bob Snodgrass, editor Steve Cameron, designer Randy Breeden and assistant Diana Rose – who all did a great job of guiding this book into print. Also special thanks to Chip Power, Steve Maxon, Dennis LaVia, and Frank Rosenberg.

Then, of course, there's my wife Karen and children Jenna, Henry and Morgan, who make the most special contributions of all.

I want to acknowledge the work of the dozens of writers who have covered the NBA, including Mitch Albom, Terry Armour, Lacy J. Banks, Jesse Barkin, Terry Boers, Clifton Brown, Bryan Burwell, Greg Boeck, Kelly Carter, Mitch Chortkoff, David Dupree, Roscoe Nance, Robert Falkoff, Bill Gleason, Bill Halls, Scott Howard-Cooper, Mike Imrem, Melissa Isaacson, John Jackson, Paul Ladewski, Bernie Lincicome, Bob Logan, Jay Mariotti, Kent McDill, Corky Meinecke, Mike Mulligan, Skip Myslenski, Glenn Rogers, Steve Rosenbloom, Eddie Sefko, Gene Seymour, Sam Smith, Ray Sons, Paul Sullivan, Mike Tulumello, Mark Vancil, Bob Verdi, Mark Heisler, Teddy Greenstein and many, many others. Their work has been invaluable.

Extensive use was made of a variety of publications, including the *Baltimore Sun, Basketball Times, Boston Globe, Chicago Defender, Chicago Tribune, Chicago Sun-Times, Daily Southtown, The Detroit News, The Detroit Free Press, Esquire, GQ, The Daily Herald, Hoop Magazine, Houston Post, Houston Chronicle, Inside Sports, Los Angeles Times, The National, New York Daily News, The New York Times, New York Post, The Charlotte Observer, USA Today, The Oregonian, Philadelphia Inquirer, San Antonio Express-News, Sport, Sports Illustrated, The Sporting News, Street & Smith's Pro Basketball Yearbook,* and *The Washington Post.*

Bob Snodgrass
Publisher

Steve Cameron
Managing Editor

Brad Breon
Publishing Consultant

Susan Storey
Assistant Editor

Randy Breeden
Art Direction/Design

Dust jacket and soft cover design by
Jerry Hirt

Production Assistance: Diana Rose,
Sharon Snodgrass, Chip Power

Select photos courtesy of the Chicago Bulls and NBA Photos

© Copyright 1996 by Roland Lazenby,
Addax Publishing Group and the Chicago Bulls.

All rights reserved.

No part of this book may be reproduced in any form without written permission from the publisher.

Published by Addax Publishing Group, Lenexa, Kansas
Printed and bound in Canada

Distributed to the trade by
Andrews & McMeel, 4900 Main Street,
Kansas City, Missouri 64112

Library of Congress Catalog Card Number: 96-085190

ISBN: 0-886110-09-3 (Limited Edition, Hardback)
ISBN: 0-886110-10-7 (General Edition, Paperback)

Contents

Foreword by Phil Jackson

T IS A GREAT HONOR TO HAVE BEEN the coach of the 1995-96 Chicago Bulls, and it is with both pride and humility that I welcome you to this retrospective on our 72-win season.

Throughout the season and the playoffs, I was asked by reporters to compare our basketball club to the other great teams of the past: the great Lakers and Celtics and Knicks and '76ers of yesteryear.

I was also asked to stack this 1996 Bulls team up against the earlier Chicago versions that won three straight NBA titles between 1991 and 1993. We had very good teams, terrific basketball clubs in those years. The 1991 team that went through the playoffs at 15-2 was remarkable, and it just continued on the next season, going 67-15.

This 1996 Bulls team didn't quite have the depth at the power positions as the other Chicago clubs, but it had the defensive notion and the offensive ability. It was a little more explosive as a basketball club because Scottie Pippen's now a much more mature three-point shooter. Michael Jordan returned to form as a confident, consummate performer night in and night out. And this time around he didn't feel the need to chase the scoring every night just because he was challenging his opponents, or out to make a great show for his fans.

And how could you replace Dennis Rodman's rebounding? Another very special touch came from the heart and grace displayed by Ron Harper, not to mention his outstanding play in the postseason. Then there was Luc Longley, always working to get better, always willing to suffer the criticism of coaches and teammates. And we had a very unusual bench player in Toni Kukoc, who has terrific talents that are adjustable between guard and forward. Beyond that we had a bench that was willing to form a role and play a part, meaning that any one of those guys – Steve Kerr, Bill Wennington, Jud Buechler, Randy Brown, James Edwards, John Salley, Jason Caffey, or Dickey Simpkins – could perform well and help the team on a given night.

There's no question that this combination has made this team very unique, one capable of the drive to win 72 games.

Does that mean we are the best of all time?

First, let me say that we have established the standard for greatness with our 72-win season. Whoever wants to better it will have to chase us.

As for the great teams of the past, I would love to put our guys on the floor against those teams, and I would be confident of the outcome. But in reality, you can't accurately compare across the decades because the game and the athletes have changed so much.

What I do feel about the honor of an historic season is that it calls to memory other great seasons, so that our accomplishment honors all the great teams of the past. Because our players were so motivated and so dominant, they have sent fans and journalists to the history books looking for teams that might beat us.

Thus we are reminded of the great George Mikan amd his Laker teams of the '40s and '50s, the truly dominant Celtics with Bill Russell, the 1967 Philadelphia club and its deep roster, the 1972 Lakers of Jerry West and Wilt Chamberlain, the Celtics of Larry Bird and Lakers of Magic Johnson and Kareem Abdul-Jabbar – and all the other championship winners from 50 years of NBA competition.

Let's just say that we are honored to take our place among that select few. Unless, however, somebody invents a time machine. Then I think maybe I could convince Michael and these guys to lace up their sneakers to settle the issue once and for all.

DENNIS, SCOTTIE, MICHAEL AND PHIL WITH THE COMPANY HARDWARE.

Introduction

T WILL ALL BE OVER BY THE TIME you read this. The confetti and trash will have been swept up in Grant Park. The sticky sweetness of spilled celebratory beverages will have been mopped from the city's floors. Even the emotion will have been put away, the yelling, the crying, the laughing, the screaming, the unmitigated glee, the ineffable joy of the whole damn thing will have passed, leaving in its wake the sweetest little tingle of indescrible feeling in your heart, a feeling that you'll keep for many years to come, a feeling that you'll want to

JORDAN WITH THE FINGER ROLL TOUCH.

JORDAN MET THE KNICKS MUSCLE WITH MAGIC.

share with your grandkids.

"There was this team," you'll tell them. "And there was this player…"

There was a city, too. And a special time and a special place.

How will you describe it for them? How do you describe magic? Better yet, how do you hold onto it?

The answer may lie in the numbers, strangely enough. They're so unbelievable that years from now they will still bear repeating.

72-10!

You may be 65 years old on a street corner somewhere, waiting for a signal to change, or

RODMAN HELPED LONGLEY BECOME A PRESENCE.

sitting on an airplane, waiting to take off, stranded in one of life's countless throwaway moments, and suddenly the whole thing will leap right from your heart.

72-10!

Aaaannnd Now… Your Four-Time World Champion Chicago Bulls!

72-10!

Michael Jordan!

Dennis Rodman!

Phil Jackson!

Scottie Pippen!

Toni Kukoc!

Jack Haley!

Jack Haley?!???

Yes, Jack Haley, sitting on the bench for 81 games until he finally got to play in game number 82, is part of the story of the greatest team ever, the 1995-96 Chicago Bulls.

They came to life in the year of the great surprise, when Michael Jordan reconfirmed the supremacy of his competitiveness, showing that contrary to what many feared, he was still able to lord over the game at age 33, still able to execute his show-stopping dunks while evolving into the sport's deadliest jump shooter.

It was also the year the circus came to town, when Dennis Rodman rebounded like Bill Russell and gave his jersey to the crowd every night, when he stopped traffic on the Kennedy

THE BULLS WERE AN INTIMIDATING PRESENCE.

THEIR DEFENSE TOOK APART EVEN THE BEST OPPOSITION.

JACKSON SAT BACK TO DO HIS COACHING.

and electrified the entire city, maybe the nation, maybe the world, with neon hairdos and tattoos and defense and body piercings and rebounds, rebounds, rebounds, and, yes, even a feather boa.

And it was the year when Scottie Pippen made peace with management and stepped forward to solidify his credentials as the game's best all-around player.

The year of the Big Heart, when Ron Harper fought off age and pain with hard work and conditioning, and became the unknown MVP, who struggled through one last night of anguish to deliver title number four.

And the year of gestalt, when Phil Jackson grew his beard and relaxed on the bench with a smile and sold his players on the idea that the power of their unity exceeded the sum of their individual brilliance.

All of these things together – Jordan's burning drive, Rodman's zany love of the game and the spotlight, Pippen's stoic leadership, Jackson's gestalt, Ron Harper's comeback, Toni Kukoc's reluctant sacrifice

and the bench's elevated play – combined to make it the year of the Great Bull Run, when Chicago's basketball team rolled across the landscape, drawing crowds and converts in every city, stirring up a storm of interest like the National Basketball Association had never seen before.

The Bulls rolled out of the gate in November to five straight wins, dropped a game to Orlando, then lost another on a six-game Western road trip to finish the month 12-2. December passed at 13-1, and when they burned their way through January at 14-0, Jackson began talking openly of resting players just to lose a few games and slow things down. But the juggernaut pushed on, finishing February at 11-3, March at 12-2 and April at 10-2. From there, Jackson refired the engines for an astounding 15-3 play-off finish, leaving the opposition quite dazed and breathless.

"He's the baddest dude to ever lace up a pair of sneakers," Orlando's Nick Anderson said of Jordan after he scored 45 points in Game 4 of

the Eastern Conference finals to complete the Bulls' playoff sweep of the Magic.

"I love the way this Chicago Bulls team plays basketball," said Seattle coach George Karl after watching Jordan and company move the Sonics aside to claim the 1996 NBA title, 4-2, the championship that validated their great run.

When it was finally over, on Father's Day 1996, Michael clutched the game ball and retreated to the locker room, where he collapsed on the floor, weeping in sadness and joy, sadness for the loss of his father, joy for the love of his children.

"I've been very blessed," Jordan later said. "That's one of the reasons I'm going to soak it up. I know I'm coming to the end of my career and still competitive, but I better enjoy every moment because you never know when it's going to end."

72-10!

Numbers that you'll want to keep for future generations.

"There was this team," you'll tell them. "And there was this player…"

THE RESULTS SPOKE FOR THEMSELVES.

AGIC JOHNSON, THE GREAT LOS Angeles Lakers point guard, was once asked to describe how it felt to lose in the postseason. "It's a hurtin' thing," he replied.

With the National Basketball Association serving as something of a domain for shared experience, it seems perfectly suitable to appropriate Johnson's description to convey the feelings of the Chicago Bulls following their loss to the Orlando Magic in the 1995 NBA Playoffs.

It was a hurtin' thing. For many reasons.

First, it hurt because the loss rather rudely punctured the city of Chicago's euphoria over the unexpected return of Michael Jordan to pro basketball. After all, His Airness was king of the city, the man who had led the Bulls to three straight NBA championships from 1991 to 1993. He had retired from basketball abruptly in '93 to try his hand at professional baseball, and just as abruptly, he decided to return to the Bulls in March 1995.

Jordan's reappearance in uniform ignited tremendous expectations. Surely Michael would resume his miraculous, high-flying style and lift the Bulls to yet another championship, despite the fact that he had played only 17 regular-season games and had been away from the sport for nearly two years.

For sure, Jordan did treat the fans to some rather stunning performances over the spring of 1995, but he also faltered with uncharacteristically clumsy moves in key moments against the Magic. Who could forget his last-minute turnover that cost the Bulls Game 1 of the series?

A similar collection of gaffes in the final minutes of Game 6 helped seal the Orlando victory

Andrew D. Berstein/NBA photo

GRANT WAS TRIUMPHANT ON THE BULLS HOME FLOOR IN 1995.

A LAST MINUTE TURNOVER IN THE 1995 PLAYOFFS MOTIVATES THEN #45 MICHAEL JORDAN TO RECOMMIT TO HIS #23 FORM.

and left Bulls fans stung by disappointment.

What made the loss worse was that the Bulls' primary executioner was Horace Grant, who had played power forward on Chicago's three championship teams, the same Horace Grant who had frequently clashed with Jordan and later departed the Bulls to join Orlando as a free agent after reneging on a handshake agreement which led to a nasty public exchange of accusations and insults with Bulls chairman Jerry Reinsdorf.

In preparing to defend Orlando center Shaquille O'Neal, Bulls coach Phil Jackson had decided to double-team Shaq while leaving Grant unguarded. It was a logical move. The rest of Orlando's starters were deadly three-point shooters. Jackson figured that leaving Grant open would mean that if he made shots, they would only be two-pointers.

Logical as it seemed, Jackson's move backfired. Grant, who always felt that he had been disrespected during his playing days in Chicago, took umbrage and answered Jackson's strategy by scoring early and often, a performance that further emphasized Chicago's weakness at power forward. The final insult came when the Magic closed out the series on the Bulls' home floor. The young Orlando players hoisted Grant to their shoulders and carried him off in celebration.

Ouch.

When Reinsdorf saw how happy Grant was that day, he tipped his hat to him. But he wasn't about to congratulate him because the two weren't on speaking terms. "I know one of his thoughts was that he had stuck it to me," the Bulls chairman said.

Bad as all this seemed, the loss hurt most because the Bulls' coaching staff studied tapes of the series and came away with the firm conclusion that Chicago could have, should have, won the series and possibly even swept it.

"We should have won all six games," assistant Jim Cleamons said of the 4-2 outcome. "The reality of it was we didn't win, but we weren't that far from winning. We lost games at the end of the clock, on last-second shots and turnovers, matters of execution.

"Good teams close the doors. They end the case. The teams that are trying to become good

JERRY KRAUSE AND PHIL JACKSON CONFER BEFORE THE 1995-96 SEASON BEGINS.

teams have those straggling situations, those dangling participles, if you will. They just don't quite get the job done."

Strange as it seemed, the Orlando loss left the Bulls realizing that they now resided in the latter category: a team trying to become good. It wasn't a status they wanted to inhabit very long. "The day after we were out of it we started planning for next year," Reinsdorf said.

The only acceptable goal would be winning the team's fourth NBA championship.

One critical aspect of that would be re-establishing a homecourt advantage in Chicago. For years, that had been a foregone conclusion when they played in the creaky old Chicago Staduim, the "Madhouse on Madison," whose thundering crowds and intimidating acoustics had hammered many an opponent into submission. But the Stadium was now headed toward life as a parking lot, having been razed to make way for the United Center, the fancy new building just across Madison that the

Bulls had spent $175 million constructing with the Blackhawks.

Brand new when the 1994-95 season opened, the United Center was the "New Madhouse on Madison," a snazzier, high-tech version of the old barn. But then the Magic had won two playoff games in Chicago, and team officials figured part of the 1995-96 challenge would be re-establishing home-court advantage.

In the aftermath of the 1994-95 season, Chicago's sports talk show airwaves were filled with anguished calls for changes, particularly for ditching the triple-post offense, the Bulls' offensive scheme pioneered by veteran assistant coach Tex Winter. The offense had played a large role in the team's three championship seasons, but now even the 73-year-old Winter expressed doubt.

In all their years of working together, Michael Jordan had never told Winter what he thought of the offense. Thus in the wake of the Orlando loss, Winter wanted to know, so he pushed Phil Jackson to discuss the issue with Jordan in the

season-ending conference.

"With his impulsiveness, Tex said, 'Phil, I'd like you to ask him, does he think we need to change the offense,' " Jackson recalled. " 'Is it something we should plan on using next year? I want you to ask him just for me.' So I did, and Michael said, 'The triple-post offense is the backbone of this team. It's our system, something that everybody can hang their hat on, so that they can know where to go and how to operate.' "

For others, the concern wasn't the offense but rather Jordan himself. It seemed pretty clear that Michael's time as the game's dominant player had passed, which meant that the Bulls' fortunes were declining as well. There was even speculation among some Bulls administrative staff members that Jordan might retire again rather than deal with the hassles of NBA life.

This speculation intensified over the summer as Jordan became involved in a battle over the collective bargaining agreement between the NBA and its players.

In years past, Jordan had failed to show the slightest interest in league labor issues, and he held a particular determination that he would never seek to renegotiate his contract with the Bulls. Yet now, here was Jordan, at the urging of his agent, David Falk, taking a leadership role in a renegade effort to decertify the union and force the league into giving its players a better deal that allowed them more freedom to negotiate contracts.

For his part, Reinsdorf had no problem with Jordan's desire to improve the opportunities for players. "It was a good business move to push for a better agreement," Reinsdorf said. "I respected that."

But the Bulls' chairman thought it was unnecessary for Jordan to hold such a high-profile role in the renegade group. Reinsdorf feared that the move would be unpopular with the fans and might hurt Jordan in the long run. "He shouldn't have been out in front," Reinsdorf said. "He could have let somebody else do that. It didn't need to be him."

Yet after the issue was over, and Jordan's side had failed in an attempt to get the agreement derailed, Reinsdorf was amazed that Jordan's popularity still bordered on a religion for many fans. "Michael is so popular, it's almost like he's Teflon. The public will forgive whatever he does," Reinsdorf said.

Despite the great public anguish over Jordan and the team's future, the Bulls coaching staff remained quietly but remarkably upbeat about their prospects. It was obvious that Orlando's talented young team would be the main contender in the Eastern Conference, and if the Bulls hoped to win another championship, they would have to rebuild their team with one purpose in mind: improving their matchups with the Magic.

Specifically, the Bulls would have to find a power forward and strengthen their post play. Plus, they would have to find bigger guards to counter Orlando's trio of Anfernee Hardaway, Nick Anderson and Brian Shaw.

With this in mind, the Bulls decided to leave veteran B.J. Armstrong, a fan favorite from the championship years, unprotected in the upcoming expansion draft. Moving quickly, the Toronto Raptors picked up Armstrong with the first pick in the draft and traded him to the Golden State Warriors in a multi-player deal.

The coaching staff didn't have to look far to find a bigger guard to replace Armstrong. Already on the roster was former all-star Ron Harper, whom Bulls vice president Jerry Krause originally had signed in 1994 to help fill the void created by Jordan's retirement.

Harper's athleticism had declined with a series of knee injuries since his days as a young superstar with the Cleveland Cavaliers, but the Bulls figured he still had promise.

"When we brought Harper in initially, we felt that if he could regain some of his old skills, his old abilities

after the knee injuries he'd had, he could be an ideal player for us because of his size," Tex Winter said.

The problem was, Harper had struggled most of the 1994-95 season to get the hang of the complicated triple-post offense, and just when he had started to come around, Jordan returned, taking most of Harper's playing time. Soon the whisper circuit around the NBA had Harper

pegged as finished, his legs gone, his game headed for mothballs.

The circumstances had left Harper understandably despondent, struggling through the lowest point in his nine-year career. "Suicide was an option," he joked. "Last season was something I learned from. It was frustrating, but my friend had a frustrating year, too," he said, referring to Pippen, who had spent much of

THE GOAL OF THE BULLS WAS TO MAKE THE UNITED CENTER A 'NEW MADHOUSE ON MADISON."

WORKING HARD AT BEING THE BEST. MANY TIMES BEFORE MICHAEL
COULD TAKE TO THE COURT FOR PRACTICE HE NEEDED TO FIND
SOMEONE THAT KNEW HOW TO TURN ON THE LIGHTS.

RON HARPER PUSHED HIMSELF THROUGH AN OFFSEASON CONDITIONING PROGRAM AND WAS READY TO STEP IN AS THE BIG GUARD THAT THE BULLS NEEDED.

yourself ready to play.' And Ron did that, he really prepared himself."

Jordan faced the same task, rebuilding his conditioning and mindset from the months of basketball inactivity, losing what Reinsdorf called his baseball body for a leaner basketball body. Jordan was scheduled to spend the summer months in Hollywood making an animated Bugs Bunny film with Warner Brothers. On another team, with another player, the coaches might have been concerned about a major summer conflict taking away from the intensity of the star player's offseason work. But this was not an issue with the Bulls coaches.

"We didn't worry about Michael," Winter said. "We figured Michael could take care of himself."

Failing his team against Orlando had been a tremendous setback for Jordan, one that bruised his giant pride. For years he had thrived on taking the Bulls' fortunes on his shoulders and lifting them with brilliant performances in front of millions of witnesses. Now he had stumbled under those same cirumstances.

"We agonized for him when he went through the postseason trauma," Jackson explained later that summer. "But knowing Michael so well, I put my arm around him after that first game in Orlando when he lost the ball and said, 'As many times as we've won behind you, I never expected to see this happen. Let's use it for our tool. Let's use it to build a positive. You're our guy, and don't ever forget that.' "

Jackson added a prediction. "Michael's not the same player," the coach said. "He's aged like everybody else has aged. But he's still Michael Jordan. He'll go back and shoot 50 percent this year, you can bet your bottom dollar on that."

Missing out on the teamwork of an 82-game season had hurt Jordan, Jackson said. "But we see Michael returning to form. When I talked to him in the postseason, I said, 'What do you see as minutes for yourself, Michael, for next year?' He said stuff

the '95 season fighting with management, "and we both grew."

Out of that growth came Harper's motivation to show everybody just how wrong they were about the status of his career.

In the wake of the Orlando loss, Jackson realized that Harper could be part of the answer and told him so in their season-ending conference.

But there was a provision: Everything hinged on Harper dedicating himself to offseason conditioning.

"Phil let Ron know that we very definitely were counting on him to be a big part of the team," Winter said. "I think that helped Ron no end. Phil put it to him in no uncertain terms: 'You gotta go out and get like 33, 35 minutes. Michael's been a 38- to 40-minute player for a lot of his career, but he sees himself coming down three to five minutes a game. But that's being realistic.

"He's a guy trying to be realistic about where he can go at this level. Michael is a guy who knows who he is. He's known that for a lot of his life. That's one of the reasons he's been able to take criticism. That's been one of the best things about his career: He's been able to take the criticism and use it to his strength."

Indeed, Jordan made it clear that the situation was his source of motivation. "The game taught me a lesson in the disappointing series I had last year," Jordan said. "It pushed me back into the gym to learn the game all over again."

For the most part, his gym had to be a temporary floor in the Hollywood studio he occupied while making his film. There, Jordan could work on his game, yet stay within reach of the film crew when he was needed to shoot a scene. A number of current and former NBA players made their way to his makeshift facility to take a spin with Jordan.

Among them was the Pistons' Grant Hill. "It was cool playing against Mike," Hill said, "and also instructive, seeing how hard he was working."

Like many others, Hill came away from the sessions thinking that people better get ready for the upcoming season. Because Mike was one determined dude.

The Bulls, though, had far more pressing concerns than Michael Jordan's return to the mountaintop.

Heading into the 1995 playoffs, general manager Jerry Krause fretted that the Bulls lacked the meanness and nastiness in the frontcourt necessary to win another championship. In their three title years, center Bill Cartwright had anchored the defense with ferocity.

Cartwright wasn't a mean person. In fact, he was something of a sweetheart off the court, but as a player he was an intimidator with a wicked set

of elbows that other teams feared.

Now that Cartwright had retired, the Bulls had come to rely on a trio of centers, Will Perdue, Luc Longley and Bill Wennington, to get the job done in the post. Perdue could block shots, Wennington had a feathery offensive touch and Longley had the huge body necessary to struggle against giants like Shaq. None of the three Chicago centers was a complete force on his own, but collectively they formed what the press had taken to calling a "three-headed monster," a patchwork solution assembled by the coaches.

Ideally, the Bulls would get a complete center to match Orlando for 1995-96. The only problem was, there just weren't any around.

"They're very special people, those dinosaurs, those elephants, those rhinoceroses, whatever you want to call those big bodies out there," Jackson said. "They're of a special value in this league."

The answer for the Bulls had been to try to develop a solid center. In this effort, Longley was their leading candidate, primarily because he was young (26), and at 7-2, 290 pounds, he had that dinosaur body to fit the specifications. But 1995 had not been a good season for him. He spent much of the year sidelined by a stress fracture, and when he did return, like Jordan, he did not have a good playoff, particularly in the clutch against Orlando. He missed a wide-open dunk in the closing sec-

HARPER SAID THAT HE AND GOOD FRIEND SCOTTIE PIPPEN HAD BOTH GROWN DURING THE DISAPPOINTING 1994-95 SEASON.

JACKSON FELT THAT
LONGLEY HAD THE
SIZE TO BE THE
BULLS' STARTING
CENTER.

onds of Game 6 that could have helped keep Chicago's season alive.

In Longley's defense, he had no solid power forward playing alongside him, and no center, not even Kareem Abdul-Jabbar, can function effectively without some solid frontcourt help.

But now, with the '95 season over, the coaches began thinking about starting again with Longley, who had come to Chicago from the Minnesota Timberwolves in a February 1994 trade for Stacey King.

"The kid's a solid worker," Jackson said in assessing Longley's upside in June 1995. "He's got a great desire to play the game. He's very intelligent. He doesn't have fear.

But he's not mean, that's one of the things that we know about him. He's not rugged mean like that. Some people think that you have to have a center that's ferocious, that threatening type of defender.

"We've found that chemistry-wise, you can build that back up. We may have to get another position player, a power forward that does have that meanness. But with Michael and Scottie, you know we have those kinds of defenders out there already. An added person is what this team needs to get back to that level of being resilient – not being bullies, not being threatening, but being resiliently tough."

The Bulls coaches figured that

with Jordan back and committed to winning a championship, with Pippen, Longley and Toni Kukoc maturing, with Ron Harper refurbishing his game, they had just about all of the major pieces in place, except for what was perhaps the most important one.

"We still needed a rebounder," Jimmy Cleamons said.

Someone to give the roster a nasty factor, someone to play defense and buck up the Bulls' courage, someone to go get the ball when the team needed a tough rebound. Players like that, of course, are very rare, but Jerry Krause had his eye on a special one.

HARPER PAID THE PRICE TO REBUILD HIS GAME.

2

FOR JACK HALEY, THE WILD RIDE began innocently enough. He was assigned a locker next to Dennis Rodman in the San Antonio Spurs dressing room. At the time, it didn't seem like such a big deal. After all, Haley's affiliation with the Spurs held little potential for a long-term relationship.

It was December 1993, and Haley had just been claimed off the waiver wire, the latest stop in a herky-jerky pro career that had seen him play for six different teams in seven seasons.

Haley, however, wasn't complaining. He was lucky to be there. Not many players who average a mere 3.7 points and 4.4 rebounds per game in college manage to make it in the NBA. Yet that's just what Haley had done after playing three unimpressive seasons at UCLA.

Figuring him for a project, the Bulls selected Haley in the fourth round of the 1987 draft because he had size and could play a little position defense. That was usually good enough for a late-round pick in the old days of the NBA's expanded draft. But Haley failed to stay long on anybody's roster.

If nothing else, his survival by the time he arrived in San Antonio had shown Haley to be quite adept at filling the role of 12th or 13th man on an NBA team. He knew how to cheer from the bench.

After six years in pro basketball, Jack Haley understood that to make it with a team, he had to establish relationships as quickly as he established his game. Sure, Rodman's troubled reputation preceded him, but Haley figured he could hit it off with anyone, even a sullen, tattooed man with dyed hair and earrings.

"I walked in," Haley recalled of that first day, "and said, 'Hey, howyadoin? I'm Jack Haley.' He wouldn't even acknowledge I was in the room or shake my hand. We sat next to each other for almost three months and never spoke a word."

Haley really wasn't all that surprised by the silence. He knew Dennis Rodman had been one of the NBA's great mysteries since the Detroit Pistons first selected him in the second round of the 1986 draft.

Although some people in the Pistons organization later claimed that Rodman was fundamentally troubled, many in Detroit simply saw him as a fun-loving, immature guy who could be surprisingly sweet. One of his favorite pastimes was hanging out with teenagers in mall game rooms –growing up in Dallas, he had gotten the nickname "Worm" from his antsiness playing pinball. He was also known for handing out big bills to the city's many street people, and one time he reportedly took a homeless man to his house, fed him, gave him a bath and handed the wide-eyed fellow $500.

This giving side was just more proof that Rodman was hardly the typical NBA player, the kind of actions that prompted former Piston teammate John Salley to say that Dennis Rodman was one of the few "real people" in the NBA.

Certainly he was unlike many other NBA players in that he had not come up through the ranks of the great American basketball machine. He had not been on scholarship his entire life, wearing the best shoes and equipment and staying in fancy hotels where the meal checks were always paid. Rodman missed all of that.

Although his two younger sisters were hoops stars in high school and college, Rodman was only 5-foot-9 when he graduated from South Oak Cliff High School in Dallas. Shy and insecure, he hadn't even played high school basketball. His only prospects after high school were a series of menial jobs. But, miraculously, Rodman's life was rescued by his pituitary. He grew 11 inches in one year, yet even that only increased his isolation.

By age 20, Dennis was 6-8 and had outgrown his clothes, leaving his only attire the oversized coveralls from his job washing cars.

RODMAN BROUGHT HIS CONTAGIOUS ENTHUSIASM TO CHICAGO.

JACK HALEY AND DENNIS RODMAN HAD BECOME CLOSE IN SAN ANTONIO.

HALEY ENJOYED TRACKING RODMAN'S OUTRAGEOUS IMAGE.

About the only place he didn't feel like a geek was the playgrounds. Pickup basketball became his refuge, and his height was one of his first real advantages in life.

It was one of his sisters' friends who got him a tryout at Cooke County Junior College in nearby Gainesville, Texas. He played there briefly, dropped out, then wound up at Southeastern Oklahoma State, where he used his size and quickness to become something of a force in NAIA basketball, averaging nearly 26 points and 16 rebounds over the next three seasons, all of which prompted the Pistons to select Rodman with the 27th pick in the 1986 draft, the next giant step in his amazing transformation.

Former Pistons coach Chuck Daly recalled that Rodman's first efforts in training camp were rather disappointing, but he recovered and soon found a place in the league by focusing on playing defense and rebound-ing. He performed these chores so well that he became a key figure as the Pistons claimed back-to-back league titles in 1989 and '90.

To accomplish goals as a player, Rodman had come to rely on a natural hyperactivity that supercharged his frenetic playing style. "My friends knew I was hyper. Real hyper," he once said of his days growing up in Dallas. "They knew I wouldn't settle down, I wouldn't sleep. I'd just keep going. And now I just focus my energy in something I love to do. Now, I just play basketball, go out there and have a lot of fun and enjoy."

This joy was obvious in his gait. In warmups, he would run erect, proudly springing off each toe, then kicking his heels up behind him almost daintily. But there was nothing sissified in the way he played.

Back in the netherworld of Dallas, Dennis had worked briefly pounding fenders in an auto body shop. And he was certainly willing to bang, body and board in the NBA. Rodman's enthusiasm for mixing it up complemented his natural athleticism and a surprisingly studious approach to all types of shot angles. A young man with an unrefined offensive game, Dennis knew from the beginning that he had to develop other skills to thrive, and he certainly did that.

After watching him in the 1989 Finals, Lakers broadcaster Chick Hearn declared that Rodman was the NBA's best rebounder. Hearing that, Rodman was stunned. "The best rebounder?" he asked. "In the game? You mean they put me in front of Oakley, Barkley, all those guys?"

At Daly's suggestion, Rodman had made rebounding and defense his

RODMAN'S BAD BOY IMAGE MEANT THAT MOST NBA TEAMS WERE LEERY OF SIGNING HIM.

RODMAN IS AN ALMOST INCESSANT WEIGHT LIFTER.

BULLS CHAIRMAN JERRY REINSDORF OKAYED GENERAL MANAGER JERRY KRAUSE'S EFFORTS TO TRADE FOR RODMAN.

mission after the 1987 playoffs. "I just came to training camp and said, 'Hey, I want to play defense,' " Rodman recalled. "Then the 1988 playoffs really got me going. I just told myself, 'It's time to start focusing on something you really want to do.' I just feel like defense is something I really want to do."

Daly, of course, couldn't have been more pleased. Rodman moved into the starting lineup for 1989-90 and helped the Pistons win another championship. It was during this period, as the Pistons shoved aside Jordan and the Bulls in the playoffs for three straight seasons, that fans in Chicago came to absolutely despise Rodman, Bill Laimbeer and all the other Piston Bad Boys.

Eventually, however, Detroit's guard-oriented offense declined. The Pistons were swept by Chicago in the 1991 playoffs, and although Detroit made a playoff run in 1992, Daly moved on to coach the New Jersey Nets, leaving Dennis without the fatherly coaching connection he needed.

Besieged by personal and off-court problems, Rodman let his frustra-

tions build, leading to clashes with Pistons coaches and management.

In October of 1993, the Pistons traded Rodman to the Spurs, thus igniting the next amazing stage in the transformation of Dennis Rodman. From all accounts, he came to San Antonio a changed man. As Rodman explained it, "I woke up one day and said to myself, 'Hey, my life has been a big cycle. One month I'm bleeding to death, one month I'm in a psycho zone.' Then all of a sudden the cycles were in balance."

This new "balance" left him searching through a series of tattoo shops, piercing pagodas, alternative bars and hair salons to find the new Dennis, the one with the electric hair. The old Dennis, however, still played basketball like a wild man.

Jack Haley watched in amazement that winter of 1994 as Rodman moved in and silently took control of the power forward spot in San Antonio, giving Spurs center David Robinson the kind of help that he'd never enjoyed before. Soon Rodman was regularly pulling down 20 rebounds a game, an astounding feat.

"I figured they were padding his

KRAUSE, JACKSON AND RODMAN ANNOUNCED THE TRADE IN OCTOBER.

stats," Haley said. "I figured no one could get 20 rebounds a night. So I started counting his rebounds. I'd come to him in a game and say, 'You got 17. You need three more.' Or, 'You need two more.' Or, 'You're having an off night. You only got five.' One game, he said to me, 'How many rebounds do I have?' From there, we developed a slow dialogue."

Perhaps it was the fact that Haley is one of the least threatening people in the NBA. Perhaps it was the fact that he was patient, that he made a low-key effort. Whatever it was, this casual acceptance somehow accelerated into a full-blown friendship about midway through the seson.

Indeed, Haley found he could hang rather easily on Rodman's zany planet, among his offbeat circle of friends, including a growing number

of celebrities, models, hairdressers, coin dealers and whoever else happened to nudge their way into Rodman's presence.

Before long, though, the Haley-Rodman relationship became apparent to those around them. They had the simplest yet strongest of bonds. They needed each other.

Haley needed Rodman to legitimize his NBA existence, and Rodman needed Haley to interpret his actions and communicate his feelings and intentions to the people he didn't want to deal with, mostly the players and management of the San Antonio Spurs. The main problem, it seemed, was that Rodman had almost nothing to say to his teammates, particularly superstar David Robinson.

Rodman seemed intent on living by his own rules, being late to prac-

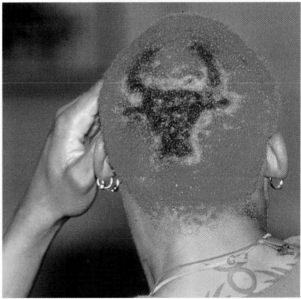

tices and games, wearing bizarre clothing and jewelry in practices and generally violating much of the protocol that had been established for pro basketball teams over the decades. Spurs coach John Lucas had

RODMAN CAME TO CHICAGO WITH THE BULLS CLEARLY ON HIS MIND.

SOME QUESTIONED WHETHER RODMAN AND PIPPEN COULD PLAY TOGETHER.

decided the best way to keep Rodman happy and motivated was to allow him to live by a different set of rules than the rest of the Spurs, which is to say almost no rules at all.

When Rodman acted up in the 1994 playoffs, and the Spurs lost to the Utah Jazz, the policy of appeasement cost Lucas and general manager Bob Bass their jobs. Next San Antonio brought in general manager Gregg Popovich, who had a military background, and coach Bob Hill with the idea that they would provide a more structured, disciplined system to keep Rodman in check.

Dennis, however, rebelled against these tighter regulations. Mainly, though, he was angry because he believed the team had promised to rework his contract because it paid him less than many of the substitutes on the team. When Rodman balked at playing under his old contract, the

team suspended him to start the 1994-95 season. Finally, after missing six weeks' pay, Rodman agreed to give the team his best effort, an immense relief to coach Bob Hill.

"Defensively, if you just take a tape and watch him, his instincts for knowing where the ball is all the time are incredible," Hill said shortly after Rodman rejoined the team. "He just always knows where the ball is. I think that's one of the reasons he's such a good rebounder. He plays great position defense. He's always ready to help. If you get one guy doing that, that's contagious for the team. They start helping one another and trusting one another defensively. That's when you win games."

The Spurs won plenty of games over the winter and spring of 1995, but Rodman's differences with management dogged the team like a running skirmish. The Spurs had their

rules, and Rodman answered with an insurrection that cost him tens of thousands of dollars in fines.

Rodman's disruptions continued right through the 1995 playoffs, where the Spurs advanced to the Western Conference finals against Houston. But enraged by behavior it called detrimental to the team, Spurs management suspended Rodman for the pivotal fifth game in the series. San Antonio lost that game and the next, eventually falling 4-2 to the Rockets.

Immediately afterward, Spurs management began looking around to see if someone would take their Dennis the Menace in a trade.

San Antonio, though, had trouble finding takers for an expensive 35-year-old eccentric. Rodman's ideal scenario was to get with another team for the last year of his contract, perform well and sign a new two- or

THE BULLS HELD TRAINING CAMP AT THE BERTO CENTER IN DEERFIELD.

RODMAN SHOWED CHICAGO FANS THAT HE WAS THE NBA'S FIRST TRUE CHAMELEON.

three-year deal in the neighborhood of $15 million.

"I'll put $5 million in the bank, live off the interest and party," Rodman told reporters – just the kind of talk that made NBA general managers very nervous.

One executive who remained intrigued by Rodman was Bulls vice president Jerry Krause, who was thoroughly familiar with Rodman's special abilities. Actually, Krause said, it was his assistant, Jim Stack, who kept bugging him about Rodman. "Jim Stack came to me early in the summer and asked me to look at Rodman," Krause said. "When I put him off, he finally pleaded with me. He talked me into finding out if all the bad things we had heard were true. Without Jim's persistence, we wouldn't have looked behind all the rumors to see what the truth was."

The upside was enough to keep Krause interested, so he broached the subject with boss Jerry Reinsdorf. The team chairman still simmered with contempt for the tactics of the Detroit Bad Boys, and Rodman had been a prominent perpetrator. Yet Reinsdorf wasn't surprised when Krause came to him about the possibility of getting Rodman.

"We had actually talked about Dennis a year earlier," Reinsdorf said, explaining that the Bulls had considered trading for Rodman in 1995. "So I wasn't shocked. Rodman had to be available. When Jerry came to me and said a deal could be made and it was one we could live with, I thought it was worth pursuing. Actually I thought it was a great idea as long as he didn't play dirty and Jerry and Phil (Jackson) could satisfy themselves that he was a good bet not to self-destruct.

"I didn't know Dennis. I only knew about the stories, like sitting in a parking lot with a gun in Detroit and the problems he had with other teams. I told Jerry that if you can satisfy yourselves that it's a good risk, then I'm all for it, because we need

to rebound the ball better. But I wanted he and Phil to be sure that the odds were with us, so that's why they spent a great deal of time talking to Dennis."

The league's labor troubles over the summer of 1995 required a moratorium on all trades and con-

tract moves, which meant that Krause had time to conduct a thorough background check. Friends, enemies, former coaches, former teammates – the Bulls contacted a wide range of people.

Encouraged by what he heard, Krause invited Rodman to come to

RODMAN MADE AN IMMEDIATE IMPACT WITH KEY REBOUNDS.

DENNIS UNDER WRAPS ON THE TEAM PLANE DURING A ROAD ALL-NIGHTER.

ON THE ROAD WITH THE BULLS.

didn't know sometimes.

"The very first preseason game of the year," Haley said, "Dennis goes in the game, Dennis throws the ball up in the stands and gets a delay-of-game foul and yells at the official, gets a technical foul. The first thing I do is I look down the bench at Phil Jackson to watch his reaction. Phil Jackson chuckles, leans over to Jimmy Cleamons, our assistant coach, and says, 'God, he reminds me of me.' "

Rodman discovered that rather than fine him $500 for being late to practices, as the Spurs had, Jackson handled the matter with a light hand. Fines were only five bucks. "Here, the first couple of days, he walked in one or two minutes late," Haley said. "Nobody said anything. So once Dennis realized it wasn't a big deal, he was on time."

It was about this time, during the preseason, that veteran Chicago Sun Times columnist Lacy J. Banks predicted that the Bulls would win 70 games, which brought hoots of derision. But the seed had been planted.

Team chemistry got another boost in the second preseason game when Rodman rushed to Pippen's aid after Indiana's Reggie Miller made some threatening moves. It was clear that Dennis was going to be the kind of rebounder, defender and intimidator that Krause wanted.

"I'm looking forward to a lot of brawling around here," he told reporters. "We need brawling on this team."

While Rodman was a surprise early fit, the other factors would take time. Jordan wasn't so sure that his pairing with Harper in the backcourt was going to work, but Jackson advised patience. Harper's presence meant that Jordan was handling the ball more. With his offseason work he had regained his basketball conditioning. Michael seemed like his former self on the floor. The confidence was tangible. Pippen, too, seemed more at ease with Michael back. Pippen's private life had gone through some changes, and Jackson noticed that he

Fortunately, things seemed to take a sudden turn for the better with the Bulls' first two exhibition games. They opened play in Peoria, of all places, against the Cleveland Cavaliers, whom the Bulls defeated easily with Jordan scoring 18 points and Rodman getting 10 rebounds.

"Once he gets a little more familiar with everybody out on the floor and there's more continuity, he's going to start to shine," Jordan predicted.

Rodman was obviously thrilled to be a Bull. "People have to realize that this team is going to be like a circus on the road," he said. "Without me, it would be a circus. But Michael, Scottie and me, it's more of a circus. A lot of people want to see the Bulls again."

Indeed, Rodman's presence made the Bulls even more of a magnetic attraction, if that was possible. Yet, where Jordan and Pippen had always taken a businesslike approach to winning, Rodman brought a fan-friendly, interactive, fun-filled style to the game that always seemed to set any arena on edge. What was he going to do next?

Rodman admitted that even he

seemed more focused than ever.

At center, Luc Longley seemed eager to face the challenge of the coming season as a starter, and veteran Bill Wennington was comfortable in his role as a backup. For additional insurance in the post, Krause signed 39-year-old James Edwards, himself a former Piston and a friend of Rodman's, thus assuring that the Bulls would have post depth and the oldest roster in the league.

Krause also had brought in guard Randy Brown to work with Steve Kerr as backcourt reserves. Also coming off the bench were Jud Buechler, Dickey Simpkins and first-round draft pick Jason Caffey from the University of Alabama.

The other bubble in the mixture was Toni Kukoc's reluctance to play the sixth-man role, or third forward. He wanted to start, but his spot in the lineup had gone to Rodman. Jackson talked to Kukoc about the success that Celtic greats Kevin McHale and John Havlicek had enjoyed as sixth men, but it was not a concept that Kukoc embraced immediately.

Changing Kukoc's mind would take patience, Jackson reasoned, but there was a whole season ahead and there would be plenty of time.

The only remaining question was Rodman. Early on, his behavior had been strange but acceptable. But how long would it last?

Still, there was a special air about this team. The Bulls finished the preseason 7-1, but lost Longley for opening night due to his suspension for punching Washington's Chris Webber in the last preseason game. A picture of the incident showed big Luc tangling with Webber and his teammates while Jud Buechler stood by watching.

Longley signed the print, "To Jud, thanks for all your help," and hung it in Buechler's locker.

With that laugh, the Bulls were off and running.

IN THE LAST PRESEASON GAME, LONGLEY GOT INTO A TUSSLE WITH WASHINGTON'S CHRIS WEBBER.

THE GRIND WAS UNBELIEVABLE. IF anybody knew that, Tim Grover did.

Grover had made it his life's work to put people through the grind, to break them down with a routine and monotonous torture. He is, after all, a personal trainer. You pay your money, he gives you the grind.

Through the process, you're supposed to find out something about yourself, mainly how badly you want the success that the grind can bring you.

Some of Grover's clients want it more than others, of course. Over the long, hot summer of 1995, Grover worked with someone who wanted it more than anyone.

"I've never seen anybody work harder than Michael Jordan," Grover said. "He fulfilled his normal summer obligations —shooting commercials, making some personal appearances — and he shot a movie. But his conditioning program always remained his primary objective."

For Jordan, the torturous offseason program was just the beginning to a year-long effort to regain the dominance he had enjoyed in the NBA as a younger man.

Now, he was nearing his 33rd birthday, trying to prepare himself to face not only the game's talented young players but the spectre of his own legendary youth. No matter what he did as an aging comeback player, he would have trouble measuring up to the standard he had set from 1986 to 1993, when he overshadowed the league.

Jordan led the NBA in scoring for seven straight seasons and drove the Bulls to three straight world championships. Now, the older Michael Jordan was taking on the younger, magical version. He began this quest with the grind.

"I'm the kind of person who thrives on challenges," Jordan explained, "and I took pride in people saying I was the best player in the game.

"But when I left the game, I fell down in the ratings. Down, I feel, below people like Shaquille O'Neal, Hakeem Olajuwon, Scottie Pippen, David Robinson and Charles Barkley. That's why I committed myself to going through a whole training camp, playing every exhibition game and playing every regular-season game. At my age, I have to work harder. I can't afford to cut corners. So this time, I plan to go into the playoffs with a whole season of conditioning under my belt."

Such drive had become the motor of Jordan's game over the past six seasons. His intensity was first pushed to that rare level by the Bulls' confrontations with the Pistons in the Eastern Conference playoffs between 1988 and 1990.

The worst, by far, was Chicago's humiliating loss in Game 7 of the conference finals in Detroit in 1990. Furious with his teammates, Jordan cursed them at halftime, then sobbed in the back of the team bus afterward. "I was crying and steaming," he recalled. "I was saying, 'Hey, I'm out here busting my butt and nobody else is doing the same thing. These guys are kicking our butt, taking our heart, taking our pride.' I made up my mind right then and there it would never happen again. That was the summer that I first started lifting weights. If I was going to take some of this beating, I was also going to start dishing out some of it. I got tired of them dominating me physically."

With that motivation, Jordan carried the Bulls to their three straight championships,

MICHAEL, THE CONSUMMATE PRACTICE PLAYER.

JORDAN WAS EAGER TO PROVE THAT HE WAS STILL A FORCE.

JORDAN HAD A LOT OF THINGS ON HIS MIND FOR 1995-96, INCLUDING PLENTY OF TICKET REQUESTS.

and during the ride often used his fierce competitiveness to drive his teammates as well. Now, in the process of trying to revive his game, he had turned again to that motivation.

Michael had returned from minor-league baseball in the spring of 1995 to find a Bulls roster full of new faces. And that had proved to be almost as much of an adjustment as his conditioning. He seemed closer to Pippen, but his relationships with his newer teammates seemed strained. Some of them thought he was aloof, unless they happened to elicit his competitive anger. Then they felt a singe.

"He knows he intimidates people," Phil Jackson said of Jordan. "I had to pull him in last year when he first came back. He was comfortable playing with Will Perdue. He was tough on Longley. He would throw passes that, at times, I don't think anybody could catch, then glare at him and give him that look. And I

MICHAEL WAS DETERMINED TO ANSWER ALL QUESTIONS FOR 1996.

let him know that Luc wasn't Will Perdue, and it was all right if he tested him out to see what his mettle was, but I wanted him to play with Luc because he had a big body, he wasn't afraid, he'd throw it around, and if we were going to get by Orlando, we were going to have to have somebody to stand up to Shaquille O'Neal."

Jordan tempered the fire directed at his new teammates without banking his competitiveness. Instead, he refocused it to drive his offseason conditioning fervor and weightlifting. He knew that he would need the added strength during the 1995-96 season to overcome the nagging injuries that accompany age. Yet even there, he had an edge.

"Between games, Jordan can bounce back from injuries that would sideline other players for weeks," Bulls trainer Chip Schaefer pointed out. "He has a remarkable body."

Michael's potent capacity for recovery, his restraint with teammates, and his unique commitment eventually amazed the many witnesses to his 1995-96 performances, beginning with the very first tipoff.

He scored 42 points on opening night in a victory over the Charlotte Hornets at the United Center, setting in motion a momentum that would carry his team to five straight wins, the best start in club history.

In retrospect, it seems almost ludicrous even to note such a thing. It was a season of incredible starts, with the Bulls seemingly setting a new record each week. Yet the opening night outburst was a message: I'm all the way back.

Jordan repeated it in the third game, scoring 38 points against the Toronto Raptors, including eight in a critical 15-0 fourth-quarter run.

Sensing he had latched on to a whirlwind, Rodman told reporters, "We're mean here. In San Antonio, we had guys who liked to go home and be breast-fed by their wives."

Rodman's flamboyance and wise-cracking somewhat obscured the

JORDAN HAD THE BODY TO WITHSTAND THE RIGORS OF NBA COMPETITION.

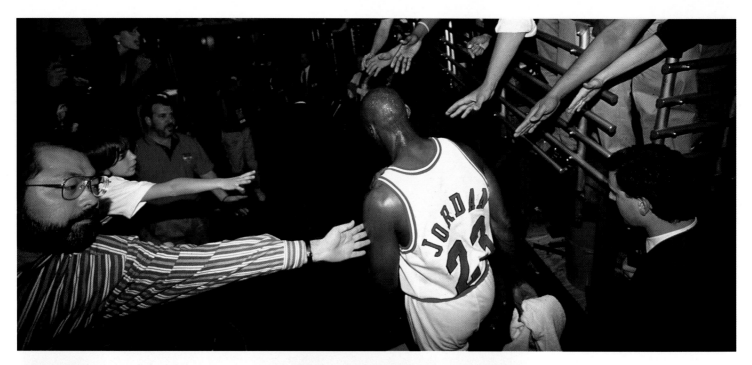

dramatic nature of Jordan's early efforts. Yet no sooner had Rodman started to settle in with the Bulls than a calf muscle injury sidelined him for a month. The injury came before their fourth game, in Cleveland, when Rodman collapsed during practice. "We were just shooting around," Jordan told reporters. "I didn't even know what happened."

Even with Rodman out of the lineup, Jordan continued on his tear, scoring 29 that night to beat Cleveland and 36 two nights later to derail Portland, 110-106. Chicago and the Trail Blazers had been tied at 100 with 2:28 left, but Michael scored six quick points in an 8-0 run to finish it.

It was in these late runs to win games that his conditioning was paying off, and each time it would happen over the coming weeks, he would think of his summer grind.

If the five quick wins did anything to dull Jordan's sense of purpose, the Orlando Magic were there with a reminder in the sixth game, just as the Bulls were breaking in their new black road uniforms with fancy red pinstripes. Penny Hardaway outplayed Michael, giving the Magic a

EVERYWHERE HE GOES, FANS REACH OUT.

key home victory.

The Bulls responded with two quick wins back in Chicago before embarking on a western road trip that required them to play seven games in 12 days. To pass the time, Jackson assigned his players books to read. Jordan was given the life story of Shoeless Joe Jackson, and backup center Bill Wennington got "Dirty White Boys," by Stephen Howard. For Steve Kerr, it was Tony Hillerman's "A Thief of Time."

The trip opened in Dallas, where the Bulls needed overtime and 36 points from Jordan (including six of the final 14 points) to win, 108-102. Jimmy Jackson missed a wide-open gimme at the buzzer that could have nailed the Bulls in regulation, but the shot fell off, giving Chicago's great early run just one more nudge.

"As far as I'm concerned, he's still one of the best in the game," the Mavericks' Jason Kidd said of Jordan. "He still finds a way to win."

Up next was San Antonio, where Rodman had hoped to play to entertain his old fans, but the calf muscle still wasn't ready. Instead, Jordan did the trick, scoring 38 with nine rebounds and four steals.

Two nights later, the challenge was Utah and Karl Malone, incredibly tough at home and boasting a six-game winning streak. Jordan scored 15 of his 34 points in the fourth quarter to whip the Jazz, 90-85.

"They have two great defenders in Pippen and Jordan, the best in the business," said Utah coach Jerry Sloan, who himself epitomized defensive intensity during his playing career with the Bulls.

"This is a very aggressive basketball club and very confident," Jackson said afterward. "I think people are surprised who we are, or are surprised how we are playing, or they're not comfortable with our big guard rotation. It's giving us some easy offensive opportunities so we're getting going early."

They got going early two nights later against Seattle, but the Sonics

MICHAEL SHOWED HE HADN'T LOST HIS TOUCH FOR SHOW-STOPPING DUNKS.

JORDAN GOT THE SEASON OFF TO A GOOD START BY SCORING 42 AGAINST CHARLOTTE ON OPENING NIGHT.

Nathaniel S. Butler/NBA photo

MICHAEL JORDAN: ROAD WARRIOR DEPARTS FROM THE BULLS CHARTER.

ONCE AGAIN CHICAGO'S EXPECTATIONS FLOATED WITH JORDAN.

turned up the defensive pressure in the second half and handed the Bulls their second defeat, 97-92, despite 21 points and 10 rebounds from Luc Longley. Chicago shot 60 percent over the first two quarters, but then began clanging shots from the floor and the line in the second half and scored just 28 points in the final 24 minutes.

Regardless, Seattle coach George Karl was impressed. "They're going to be real interesting," he said. "I think everybody sees a championship-caliber team out there. Rodman isn't even playing for them and he will be a factor. He will add another dimension."

The next night in Portland, Jordan stole the ball from the Trail

Blazers' Arvydas Sabonis with just seven seconds left, drove the length of the floor and slammed home a 107-104 win. Michael finished with 33, while Pippen checked in with 21 points and 10 assists.

In Canada, three nights later, Jordan scored 19 points over the game's final 6:48 to stave off an upset by the Vancouver Grizzlies. The 94-88 win gave the Bulls a 5-1 record on their road trip and a 12-2 mark for the month.

On December 2, they closed out the trip at a sizzling 6-1 with Michael scoring 37 in a win over the Los Angeles Clippers.

"I feel I'm pretty much all the way back now as a player," Jordan said, reflecting on the first month of the

season. "My skills are there. So is my confidence. Now it's just a matter of me going out and playing the way I'm capable every night."

Indeed, Jordan's shooting percentage, a stellar .511 prior to his return from baseball, had dipped to just .411 during his 17-game run over the spring of 1995. Now, it had jumped back to .493. His scoring, too, was headed back up to a 30-point average from the nine-year low of 26.9 in 1995.

Having witnessed this display, Chicago columnist Lacy J. Banks put together a comparison that showed if Jordan played through the 1998 season, he would rank third on the all-time scoring list with almost 29,000 points – behind only Wilt

Chamberlain's 31,419, and Kareem Abdul-Jabbar's 38,397.

"Forget Jabbar," Jordan said when Banks asked about his staying in the game long enough to eclipse the great Laker center. "No way do I plan to play anywhere close to 20 years."

For Jordan, it was the present, not the future, that held supreme importance.

"He's right where I knew he'd be about now," Ron Harper told the writers covering the team. "And that's leading the league in scoring and pulling away from the pack. He's removing every shadow of a doubt that he's the greatest player of all time."

And it was that player – not Kareem, not Wilt, not the young guns – who provided Jordan his greatest competition. "I'm old," he admitted. "Agewise, I think I'm old. But skillwise, I think I'm still capable of playing the type of basketball I know I can play. The question (people) end up asking me the most is: How do I compare the two players, the one before baseball and the one after?

"Quite frankly, I think they are the same. It's just a matter of putting out the stats to show that they are the same. And I think by the end of the year, hopefully, you will see that it's basically the same player with two years in between.

"Right now, I'm still being compared to Michael Jordan, and according to some people, I'm even failing to live up to Michael Jordan. But I have the best chance of being him because I am him. In the meantime, I'm improving and evolving. And I'm pretty sure that I'm turning some of you guys into believers."

Andrew D. Berstein/NBA photo

PIPPEN, SHOWN HERE IN AN EARLY ROAD WIN OVER CLEVELAND, BEGAN THE SEASON IN A BLAZE.

KUKOC PUT THIS ONE DOWN IN A DEFEAT OF THE CAVS AT THE UNITED CENTER, HELPING THE BULLS TO A 12-2 NOVEMBER.

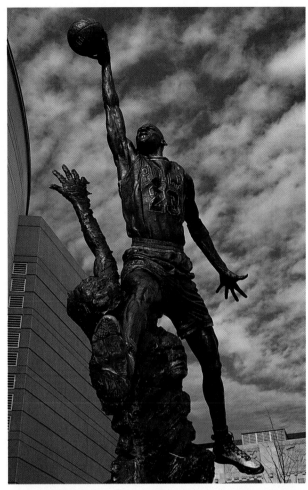

JORDAN'S TOUGHEST COMPARISON CAME AGAINST THE SPECTRE OF HIS OWN LEGEND. COULD HE MEASURE UP TO THE PAST?

4

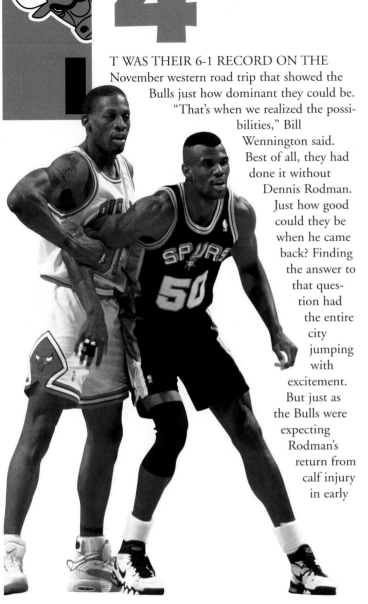

T WAS THEIR 6-1 RECORD ON THE November western road trip that showed the Bulls just how dominant they could be. "That's when we realized the possibilities," Bill Wennington said. Best of all, they had done it without Dennis Rodman. Just how good could they be when he came back? Finding the answer to that question had the entire city jumping with excitement. But just as the Bulls were expecting Rodman's return from calf injury in early

DENNIS HELPED DOMINATE HIS OLD TEAM AT THE UNITED CENTER.

KUKOC AND THE BULLS CRUISED THROUGH DECEMBER.

December, news broke about his Playboy spread. In an article accompanying his pictorial with a girlfriend, Rodman indicated that perhaps Michael Jordan and the league's other stars had been seduced by "the Pedestal," the money and fame of pro basketball.

"I bring too much excitement to the game," Rodman said. "Michael Jordan used to do that, but...now it's the Dennis Rodman show on the road."

On another team, such outrageousness could have proved devastating. The Bulls, however, shrugged it off as just another blip on their very busy media screen and kept on winning. Rodman's response was to return with

his hair dyed a bright holiday green on the sixth of December at home against New York. Driven by new coach Don Nelson, the Knicks eagerly muscled aside the Bulls to take a 56-43 halftime lead.

"A very typical Bulls-Knicks type of game," Jackson said afterward. "A lot of action, a lot of aggressiveness. We stood back and played a passive game in the first half and had to get ourselves aggressive in the third and fourth."

A big part of that aggressiveness was supplied by Rodman, who finished with 20 rebounds in 38 minutes of play, which combined with 22 points each from Jordan and Pippen and 18 from Kukoc to give Chicago a late win, 101-94.

"I thought Rodman really got the crowd going and the rest of their guys rebounding and hustling," Nelson said afterward.

Two nights later, Rodman's old team, the Spurs, came to the United Center, and he greeted them with 21 rebounds to help Chicago to a blowout, 106-87. And the night after that explosion, the victim was the Milwaukee Bucks, and again Rodman turned in 21 boards to go with a season-high 45 points from Jordan and 28 from Pippen for Chicago's sixth straight win.

Rodman had come back with a monstrous 61 rebounds in just three games, which combined with Jordan and Pippen's scoring and defense, leaving other teams depressed over the thought of trying to match up with this unique trio.

After four days rest, Chicago entertained Orlando, a team that had beaten the Bulls four straight times. This time, though, Jackson's club was ready with its best effort. Jordan poured in 36 points. Rodman snatched 19 rebounds. Pippen had 26 points. The Bulls led 61-49 at the half and pushed the lead to 20 before closing out the Magic, 112-103.

From there, the Bulls bounded on a protracted winning streak, which was accompanied by media reports marveling at Rodman's contribution to the team, at Jackson's deft coaching touch, at Jordan's renewed powers as a superstar.

Atlanta, the Lakers, the Celtics (with Jordan and Pippen scoring 37 each) and Dallas fell in order.

THEY WEREN'T EXACTLY THE THREE AMIGOS, BUT JORDAN, RODMAN AND PIPPEN FOUND THEMSELVES AT THE CORE OF SOMETHING SPECIAL.

With each victory, speculation had mounted as to whether Chicago could win 70 games, breaking the all-time record for wins in a season – set by the 1972 Los Angeles Lakers at 69-13.

Jerry West, the Lakers vice president for basketball operations who was a star guard on that '72 Los Angeles club, pegged the Bulls as stone-cold cinches to win at least 70 games unless injuries set them back.

The Bulls' success also prompted reporters to ask Jordan to compare this Chicago team to other great NBA clubs. "I look at the Celtics back in '86, back when they had Bill Walton and Kevin McHale coming off the bench," Jordan said. "Those guys were tough to deal with. Those guys played together for a long time. We're starting to learn how to play together, but those guys were together for a period of time. They knew

arms, legs, and fingers and everything about each other. We're just learning fingers."

Former Bulls assistant coach Johnny Bach pointed out that center Bill Cartwright used to stand in the back of the Bulls' defense on those championship teams, surveying the floor. In his raspy voice, Cartwright would direct his teammates to cover any open opponent. The Bulls came to rely heavily on Cartwright's direction.

"Luc Longley hasn't learned that yet," Jordan said. "If he ever learns that, it makes us really strong. If Luc learns to see the court and direct certain players, Scottie and myself, to the open people, to anchor the defense, that's very important."

Longley, an Australian who had come to the United States to play college basketball at New Mexico, could learn to do that with time,

Jordan said. "I think he's smart enough. But it takes a lot of hard work."

Even without a dominant center, the Bulls seemed to have power to spare. During their big start, they had toyed with opponents through the first two or three quarters before flexing their might and finishing strong.

"We get in that mindset where we can just go out there and beat any team," Rodman explained. "Once we see a team is really being aggressive, all of a sudden we kick in that second gear."

"From the media's standpoint, it looks like we're toying with people," Jordan said, "but for us it's just a matter of making adjustments. We may take teams for granted a little bit early in games, but then we figure them out and apply our defense where necessary in the second half."

Observers began pointing out that with expansion, the NBA had grown to 29 teams, which had thinned the talent base, making it easier on the Bulls. Those same observers conveniently forgot that the '90s talent base had been broadened by the drafting of European players and that in 1972, when the Lakers won, the American Basketball Association was in operation, meaning there were exactly 28 teams fielded in pro hoops between the two leagues.

Not only that, the NBA had just expanded dramatically before 1972, adding six teams in five years.

For the Bulls, comparisons with the Lakers and other great teams were unavoidable. And each Chicago win added to the expectations. "It's been pressure-free," Jordan said after the Dallas win, "but it won't stay that way, because right now the expectations are going to expand a little bit. It's going to start the whole 70-win chorus going again. I think Phil's going to have a tough job maintaining our focus per game so that we're not thinking about 70 wins."

Before he left the game in 1993, Jordan had frequently complained that the 82-game regular season had become a monotony. Since his return, however, he viewed it differently, and the Bulls' early success reflected that difference.

"Now, I approach it as a means of getting rhythm," he said, "getting this team to understand our chemistry, so that we understand each other, so that the fingers on the hand start to fit one another."

If there had been a dark side to the first two months of the season, it was the inconsistent play of the bench, but heading into the holidays, the reserves helped deliver two more wins, over Toronto and Utah in the United Center.

"Our bench came in and gave us what we needed," Pippen said after a 100-86 conquest of the Jazz. Wennington had scored 16 and Kukoc 11 with five rebounds. Against Toronto, Kerr had hit for 16

– including four of five three-point attempts.

Jerry Krause, Jackson and the staff had carefully arranged the pieces so that each player contributed a key element – Kukoc the offensive punch, Kerr the perimeter shot and some ballhandling, Jud Buechler the perimeter shot and defensive energy, Wennington the frontcourt scoring and defensive fouls, Randy Brown the defensive effort against smaller guards.

"The guys are playing better off

THAT DIDN'T MEAN THERE WEREN'T AWKWARD EARLY MOMENTS.

MICHAEL LED THE WAY IN A BIG EARLY COMEBACK WIN OVER NEW YORK.

the bench," Kerr said, "and it's a good thing, because we can't expect the stars to just carry us all year."

Immediately after Christmas, the Bulls traveled to Indiana, and Jordan's concerns about getting stung by an opponent's early burst finally became a reality. They fell behind by 24 points in the first half, then saw their rally fall short in a 101-94 loss that halted Chicago's 13-game winning streak.

Jackson merely suggested his team would start another streak, which they did three nights later, when the Pacers visited the United Center. The Bulls spanked Indiana 120-93 to gain a bit of retribution.

Asked about the triple-post offense, Jordan said it was a matter of the players continuing to get to know each other. As that happened, he said, the Bulls would be able to extend opposing defenses even further.

Already stretched to the breaking point, opponents around the league could only shake their heads. What would happen if the Bulls really started playing well together? Now there was a truly frightening thought.

The accolades would arrive later, but the inescapable conclusion came in December, after the Bulls had run up 13 wins against a single loss to go with their sparkling 12-2 record in November. Jerry Krause had rebuilt the Bulls yet again, and this time he had an impressive array of interchangeable parts in place around Jordan, the team's centerpiece.

Krause's efforts brought to mind the slick moves of Red Auerbach, who guided a Boston Celtics franchise that won 16 championships over four decades.

Krause held no illusions that he, or any modern NBA executive, could match the numbers that Auerbach's teams put together in the league's formative early decades. But Krause had studied Auerbach's success and admired how he had constantly shuffled and reworked the role players around Bill Russell, the

great Boston center.

To do this, Auerbach developed a knack for finding just the right rookie or pulling in an overlooked journeyman or an aging star to squeeze an effective season or two from the end of their careers.

Krause had sought similar solutions in Chicago over the past decade. There was Bill Cartwright, the offensive-minded center brought in from the Knicks to become a defensive specialist for the Bulls. As a spot-up shooter, Krause had acquired

WAS THIS REALLY SCOTTIE PIPPEN'S TEAM? JORDAN SAID IT WAS.

RON HARPER'S PLAY BECAME AN INCREASINGLY BIG FACTOR AS THE SEASON PROGRESSED.

John Paxson, then Steve Kerr and Jud Buechler. The big guards who fit in nicely included Ron Harper and Pete Myers. And he had also found a host of utility big men, including Wennington, Scott Williams, and Will Perdue, all of them contributing just enough in spot minutes.

In retrospect, these moves seemed like only a logical thing to do, but finding just the right people to fit in around Michael Jordan over the

years had required countless hours searching through the ranks of available pro and college players, scouting them, investigating their backgrounds, projecting how they would fit into the Bulls' system.

At this part of the game, Krause was relentless. Which helps explain why, as the Bulls were marching their way through an impressive season, Krause was up late nights, studying hours of videotape, or out

on the road, catching an early flight, spending hours in a rental car, driving to a remote college campus to follow up a tip on an obscure prospect.

Yet Krause persisted in these efforts because out of the hundreds of rejects, there would come to light that occasional prospect who could become part of a solution to one of the team's needs. Many times, Krause's day would end in an airport, waiting to board a late flight, where he could be accosted by a fan eager to express an opinion on the Bulls' latest personnel moves.

Krause endured these moments because he knew they came with the territory, and if nothing else was certain, Jerry Krause absolutely loved the territory. That much had been clear since his earliest involvement with sports.

The son of a Russian Jewish immigrant and merchant, Krause grew up on the north side of Chicago, in neighborhoods where he was a distinct minority, where he was called a kike and other derogatory names. Yet one of the beacons on his landscape was Jim Smilgoff, the legendary baseball coach at Taft High School.

Not only was Smilgoff a mean sonofagun and a tough competitor, he was Jewish. Needless to say, Krause idolized him. When Krause's family moved to another neighborhood, Krause decided to ride his bike eight miles each way every day so he could continue playing for Smilgoff – never mind that Krause was only a reserve catcher on the baseball team.

Krause later attended Bradley University and worked his way into a spot as the student assistant to Braves basketball coach Chuck Orsborn. His duties were to chart offensive and defensive plays, and that proved to be a major training ground for his scouting days.

Krause also managed to hang on with Bradley's baseball team, again as a backup catcher, which he discovered was a good way to get to know the big-league scouts who would hang around the batting cage quizzing warm-up catchers on the strength of a pitcher's arm.

After college, Krause worked his way into a series of baseball and basketball scouting jobs for a variety of teams. It was a hard life, 280 nights on the road each year, but Krause consumed it with relish. Later, he would joke about naming his unwritten autobiography "One

Million National Anthems."

Krause even wandered way up to the University of North Dakota in the 1960s to meet a young coach named Bill Fitch and to scout a raw-boned forward named Phil Jackson.

"Jerry Krause is an enigma to the athletic world," Jackson says now. "He's not what you would consider an athlete, and even back then, 30 years ago, he was an unusual fellow to be out there scouting a basketball player.

"But Jerry has done whatever it took to get to the top and hold his position. That's why he has such a great knowledge of the game, from A to Z. He did whatever it took, from going and getting the sandwiches and coffee, to whatever, just to keep hanging around the game and learning. And he's always been able to pick out talent. He was down there at Kansas State when Tex Winter coached there in the '60s, hanging out with Tex the way he would hang out with Bighouse Gaines at Winston-Salem State. He's always had an eye for people who are dedi-

cated to what they do."

One of Krause's first big scores was a scouting job with the old Baltimore Bullets. He dug up a fine small college player named Jerry Sloan from Evansville and later pushed to prominence Earl "The Pearl" Monroe, out of little Winston-Salem State.

Those early successes, however, didn't buy Krause much seniority. The scouting circuit was a hard road in those days, and Krause soon left the Bullets to join the Bulls in the late 1960s, shortly after they had entered the league as an expansion team. But a poor relationship with then-Bulls coach Dick Motta meant that Krause had to move on after a couple of seasons in Chicago.

The next stop was another expansion team, the Phoenix Suns.

As his reputation grew, people would marvel that Krause, obviously not an athlete himself, could be so effective as a scout. "You don't have to be a chicken to smell a rotten egg," Krause would retort.

His first really big break, or so it

STRENGTH AND CONDITIONING COACH, AL VERMEIL, WORKS WITH STEVE KERR.

seemed, came in 1976 when wily old Bulls owner Arthur Wirtz lured him back to Chicago as the team's general manager. It was quite a promotion, and it was in his hometown, which puffed up Krause with pride. Yet within weeks he got caught up in an amazingly silly turn of events.

The Bulls were looking for a coach, and DePaul's Ray Meyer told reporters that Krause had offered him the job. Krause insisted he had

done nothing of the sort, but somehow the incident got blown up into a local media firestorm. Abruptly, Wirtz fired Krause, turning his triumphant homecoming into public humiliation, and it forever shaped his view of the media.

Krause's skill as a scout meant that he quickly landed on his feet. The Lakers hired him and watched in amazement as he found them a little-known guard named Norm

Nixon. But Krause was lured back to Chicago and baseball in 1978 by White Sox owner Bill Veeck. Krause's toughness and acumen were already well-established in 1981 when Jerry Reinsdorf put together a group to buy the baseball team. The new owner soon grew to admire the plucky scout, and four years later, when Reinsdorf formed another group to buy the Bulls, Krause was his first choice to run

the organization.

"I wouldn't have taken the job had it not been for Jerry," Krause says of Reinsdorf, whom he considers a close friend. "My consideration there was not the fact that Michael Jordan was on the team. I had worked with Jerry with the White Sox for several years. I had turned down chances to come back in the NBA during that time. I had a couple of strikes against me, and I didn't want to come back unless I knew I could work for an owner I felt comfortable with and that I knew would back me and do the things that needed to be done."

Krause's basketball resurrection amazed many people, including Orlando Magic executive Pat Williams, who had known him for years. "Part of the saga of the Bulls is the incredible scent, the life of Jerry Krause," Williams said. "It's phenomenal. He starts out in Baltimore, then gets hired and fired in Chicago. So he's out and he ends up going to Phoenix. He bats around and ends up with the Lakers. He ends up working for me in Philly. He's hired back by the Bulls, and Arthur Wirtz ends up firing him after a few months on the job. He's gone, just gone, and he wheels out of that and he battles his way back and works for Reinsdorf. His life story and what happened to him is phenomenal."

JASON CAFFEY (35) AND DICKEY SIMPKINS (8) WERE THE APPRENTICE FORWARDS.

THE BULLS SILENCED
THE JAZZ IN THE
UNITED CENTER.

Perhaps Krause's two biggest moves were the hiring of veteran assistant coach Tex Winter, who designed the Bulls' famed triple-post, or triangle, offense, and the development of Phil Jackson as a NBA head coach.

Krause fired three coaches before finding the perfect leader for the Bulls in Jackson, and each firing was accompanied by a public outcry against the move, particularly the

1989 sacking of Doug Collins, who made way for Jackson.

Jackson, a bearded eccentric, had had some success in the CBA, but most NBA general managers never would have considered him head coaching material. Jackson recalled his frustration in 1985 after being named CBA coach of the year, a season after his Albany Patroons had won the CBA championship. Despite his success and his background as a

player with the New York Knicks, no NBA team expressed the slightest interest in hiring him.

"I had no mentor in the NBA," Jackson explained. "Jerry Krause was like the only person that really stayed in touch with me from the NBA world. That was my connection. Jerry had seen me play in college, and we had a relationship that spanned 20 years."

Keeping the edge to a championship

team is a difficult task, made more complex by the personalities of world-class athletes. Those circumstances often find Krause in difficult straits, such as the time he attempted to trade Scottie Pippen to Seattle over the summer of 1994. Krause said he had put together a deal with the Sonics that would have brought in power forward Shawn Kemp plus a draft pick that could have given the Bulls Eddie Jones, a bright young guard out of Temple. But at the last minute, Seattle backed out of the trade, and a series of news stories followed, revealing Krause's plans.

"The owner started getting crazy calls (from fans complaining) so the whole deal was off," Krause said. "But I put a lot of time into that, and there were a lot of things involved. If the deal had gone through, I would have wound up with Eddie Jones and that would have been real good. It bothers me...but I have been doing this for 10 years and that type of stuff happens. You've got to do what you've got to

do. Jerry was upset, and I was mad, too. I wouldn't trade Scottie unless I had a deal that I couldn't turn down."

Pippen, who was already unhappy over his contract, was further enraged that the team planned to trade him. The incident touched off a running feud between Pippen and Krause in the press that simmered for months, well into 1995, making for awkward relationships within the organization. Jackson, meanwhile thought the whole problem could have been avoided.

Reinsdorf, for his part, sees a creative tension at work in the relationship between coach and general manager, and given its success in recent seasons, it would be hard to argue against it.

"Phil gets annoyed with Jerry from time to time," Reinsdorf says. "But Jerry is Phil's boss. Everybody gets annoyed with their bosses. Back when I had bosses, I used to get annoyed with them. Whatever annoyances Phil feels, they're just

petty annoyances."

"We're a little different," Krause said of Jackson. "I'll go into a bookstore on the road, and I'll see Phil, and I guarantee you we're in different sections. But I always say, if you have two people who think the same, fire one of them. What do you need duplication for?"

Krause, who has admitted he would relish the idea of building another champion without Jordan's incredible talents, has spent a good portion of his career studying the dynasties – the New York Yankees with DiMaggio, the Dallas Cowboys, the Baltimore Orioles – looking for the similarities that made them consistent winners.

The stresses and pressures begin to add up, Krause said. "With me, a lot of them are self-inflicted. I mean, you want to do well and win. I'm unique in the sense that I'm doing it in my hometown with a job I dreamed of having, and I set my goals that I wanted to be a general

AFTER A LOSS AT INDIANAPOLIS, THE BULLS WHIPPED THE PACERS BACK AT THE UNITED CENTER, LEAVING PACERS GUNNER REGGIE MILLER LOOKING GLUM.

KRAUSE HAD GAINED HIS BASKETBALL VISION THROUGH YEARS OF SCOUTING.

KRAUSE AND JIM CLEAMONS ON THE ROAD.

THE BULLS ROLLED ACROSS THE LANDSCAPE DRAWING CROWDS AND CONVERTS IN EVERY CITY.

manager in my hometown," he said.

"I'm doing it when they all said, 'That little son-of-a-bitch can't do it.' There's a personal thing there. I get a little kick when people say how lucky I am. The harder I work, the luckier I get. The stress that I get from the reporters that sit there and write stories about me, some of it you've just got to laugh about."

With each December victory, it became harder for anyone to criticize Krause, and it became easier to find more satisfaction in the Bulls' success. Not that that lessened the self-imposed stress of his work. The road trips, the hours of searching a video monitor, the background work remained a mountain for him to climb every day. But now the team he had put together was showing incredible promise.

Just maybe, they could do things better than they had ever been done before.

RODMAN WAS THE MASTER AT GOING AFTER LOOSE BALLS.

5

WHEN IT COMES TO BASKETBALL, Scottie Pippen has been there. He was an integral part of the Bulls teams that won three straight NBA titles. He was a weapon on Dream Team I, which cruised its way to the gold medal in the 1992 Olympics. He's a perennial All-Star.

So it would seem that Pippen, when asked in January 1996 to pinpoint the most exhilarating feeling he'd ever had playing the game, would need to think a while before answering.

Instead, he didn't hesitate at the question. The most confident, powerful feeling he'd ever had, he said, was the one he was experiencing right now, as the Bulls began their march into 1996, well on their way to setting the best single-season record in league history.

The sense of power was incredible, he admitted. "Nobody figured that an NBA team could have the type of pace that we're on right now," Pippen said. "It's been a lot of fun really. Almost like a college atmosphere."

A mid-January road game against Washington offered a classic example. As Pippen emerged from the visitors' locker room at USAir Arena to make his way onto the floor for a pregame shootaround, he was greeted by a throng of fans hanging around the exit tunnel, eagerly calling his name, pushing past each other to shower him with praise and affection.

You could see the excitement spread across Pippen's normally stoic features as he walked through the fans into the arena. He'd been in the NBA for almost a decade, and you'd have thought that by now he'd have grown accustomed to the cooing and adulation. But this Bulls season was special, and the excitement in every city was just one of the reasons that, after all these years, Scottie Pippen was blushing again.

What was perhaps most remarkable about the circumstances was the team's amazing reversal of fortunes. After all, it was exactly one year prior to this magic January that Pippen had come to Washington for a road game in the midst of a very public feud with Bulls management. He was demanding to be traded and using the media to fire insults at Bulls vice president Jerry Krause.

For many in the organization, it was one of

THE FALL OF 1995 BROUGHT A NEW AND IMPROVED PIPPEN.

the lowest moments in the team's history.

Yet now, exactly one year later, Pippen's world had reversed itself. The Bulls were riding a crest, and the 6-foot-7 Pippen was off to perhaps the best start of his career. It seemed that sportswriters everywhere were suggesting that he deserved to be named the league's most valuable player. Even Michael Jordan had told reporters that the Bulls were really "Scottie's team."

"He's the leader of this team," Jordan had said in December. "Now I'm one of his supporting cast."

That statement was obviously a bit of an exaggeration, but Jordan was acknowledging not only Pippen's stellar play, but also the bur-

PIPPEN'S SMILE SAID IT ALL.

den Pippen had carried during Jordan's 18-month absence from basketball.

Like Dennis Rodman, Pippen had traveled a strange route to stardom. After limited playing experience as a 6-1 high school point guard, Pippen had gone to Central Arkansas in 1983 on a scholarship as team manager. But he had begun growing, and his role at the school quickly shifted, from manager to star.

By his senior season, he had sprouted into a long-armed NAIA All-American averaging 26 points and 10 rebounds per game, so solid a prospect that Jerry Krause engineered a series of moves in 1987 to bring him to the Bulls with the fifth overall pick of the draft.

Pippen came to Chicago as a small-town guy with a small-college background, and his adjustment to playing in the bright lights alongside Jordan took some time. Pippen, however, had the talent and the drive

to mature into a star in Chicago. His development was a key factor in the Bulls' ability to win their three straight league titles.

Pippen, however, wasn't entirely prepared for the demands placed on him with Jordan's abrupt retirement in October 1993. And who would have been? Jordan was merely the greatest player in the world.

Suddenly, Pippen had to assume the role of top offensive performer for this high-profile team, and with it came all of the additional media pressures that Jordan had borne for years.

Pippen responded with a brilliant 1993-94 season, as the Bulls ran up 55 wins without Jordan and made a strong playoff showing. But as Phil Jackson pointed out, this placed immense pressure on the former team manager from little Hamburg, Arkansas, which may help to explain some of his questionable behavior, particularly his refusal to enter Game

3 of the 1993 Eastern Conference Semifinals against the New York Knicks with 1.8 seconds left and the game on the line.

Jackson had diagramed the Bulls' last shot for Toni Kukoc, and Pippen felt it should have been his to take.

Jordan, playing baseball in Alabama, saw the game on TV and winced at Pippen's mistake. "I was totally afraid for him," Jordan said. "From that point on, he had a lot of negative things happening to him. No one had as much sympathy for him as I did."

Pippen's explanation: "I always felt life should be a certain way. I was always trying to be a perfectionist, you might say. I wanted everything to happen in a certain way, and when it didn't, I didn't handle it. Instead of doing my best and realizing that's all I could do, I was pushing."

Pippen's defenders point out that, faced with the burden of being the Bulls' top scorer, rebounder, defender and passer, Pippen had no choice but to be pushy. If he played well, the Bulls were a good team. If he didn't, the disappointment was gigantic.

The ensuing 1994 offseason brought the Bulls' failed efforts to trade Pippen for Kemp, which only added emotional pressure to the performance pressure already facing Pippen. Then the weight increased when Horace Grant, the Bulls' outstanding power forward, left as a free agent for Orlando, further weakening Chicago's roster for 1994-95.

The circumstances, Pippen conceded, offered him ample opportunities to learn some very hard lessons. One night, for example, he threw a chair onto the floor during a timeout. The incident, set off by Pippen's anger with an official, offered what he called "the highest learning experience."

"That was something that told me I was out of control," he said.

Pippen had thrown the chair because he felt the need to take a stand, yet he soon realized that it was perhaps a bigger issue than even his refusal to enter the playoff game. Public reaction again was negative, and Pippen had to confront himself.

At the same time, he was engaged in his war of words with Krause, and the situation seemed to have the Bulls headed for a painful crash.

Jordan's abrupt return in March 1995 no doubt prevented disaster. Yes, the Bulls suffered their painful loss to Orlando in the 1995 playoffs. But in the aftermath, Pippen decided he was going to take a different approach for 1995-96.

"I had made up my mind going into the season that I was just going to play basketball, have fun and enjoy the game," he said. "And enjoy what I had, instead of taking everything that happened so seriously."

Enjoying the game more meant that Pippen had to make a commitment to greater self control. Scottie felt he needed to do that just to survive the rigors and intense pressure of trying to be a great player on a great team.

As for talk of his being the league MVP, Pippen said, "It doesn't really faze me one way or the other. I feel like I've always been capable of how I'm playing right now. When you've got a guy like Michael out on the court, he really has the ability to overshadow any type of player because he's so flamboyant. I feel like I'm doing the same things I've always done on the court."

If nothing else, the near-trade to Seattle had taught Pippen just how fragile success is in the NBA. "This season is very special because there are some great players on this ballclub," he said. "I may not ever again get the opportunity to play with guys like Michael and Dennis and the guys we have on the second unit."

In particular, the opportunity to play with Jordan was something special. "I think we're much closer now than we were two years ago," Jordan said. "We spend more time together. We talk more about different things other than basketball. I think he really has a sensitivity to my life, and

HIS EARLY PLAY BROUGHT CALLS FOR HIS SELECTION AS MVP.

SCOTTIE'S LEADERSHIP WAS A KEY FOR THE BULLS.

PIPPEN AND JORDAN HAD GAINED A GREATER APPRECIATION FOR ONE ANOTHER.

I totally have a sympathy to his life. We've become friends."

Together, Jordan and Pippen comprised the most unique pair, the most difficult set of matchups in NBA history.

"Scottie's an MVP player, there's no doubt about it," Jackson said. "Michael makes him an even greater player because he doesn't have to worry about scoring to carry the team. But Michael is really the greatest player this game has produced. And the combination of the two of them in tandem, I think, has a very terrific effect upon opponents."

The Bulls' unprecedented success and his relaxed approach even brought back Pippen's sense of humor, meaning that as the Bulls kept winning, his thoughts turned to a fun-filled fantasy.

"I would like to give Phil the night off one night," he said. "Him and Tex. Maybe after we get 70 wins and have one left, Phil can take the night off. Then I would let Dennis be the coach. That will be the night we get Michael to go for 100."

The Bulls opened the New Year in style, with a 100-86 win over the

THE WEIGHT OF SCORING WAS NOT SOMETHING THAT HE ALWAYS ENJOYED.

THE BLUR OF THE SPOTLIGHT WAS NOT A COMFORT ZONE FOR SCOTTIE.

AS A MATURED TEAM LEADER, PIPPEN COULD BE ALL BUSINESS — ON AND OFF THE COURT.

Houston Rockets, the league's two-time defending champions, in the United Center. Jordan scored 38, and Chicago allowed the Rockets just one of 15 field goal attempts in the second quarter. With a 17-point halftime lead, the Bulls cruised to their 26th win.

The next night, January 4th, they traveled to Charlotte and quickly snuffed the Hornets, 117-93. Larry Johnson, Charlotte's only post threat, was held to four points.

Charlotte assistant Johnny Bach, the Bulls' former defensive coach, said afterward that he had his doubts that Jackson would allow the Bulls to break the 70-win barrier. In 1992, the Bulls were laying a similar terror on the league, Bach said, but Jackson deliberately rested his starters to make sure the team wouldn't win 70. The league office was perturbed at Jackson's manipulation of the win column. But Jackson did it to make sure the Bulls were rested enough to win the 1992 title.

Jackson acknowledged slowing the team down in '92 to get ready for the playoffs and said he would do the same in '96.

Each season presents a mystery, which is why he loved coaching, Jackson explained. "The mystery of

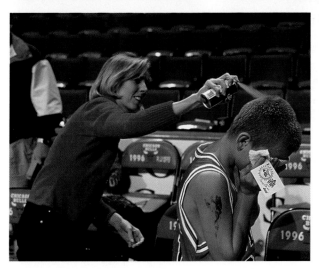

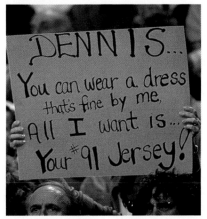

RODMAN'S WALK ON THE WILD SIDE HAD FANS ACROSS CHICAGO THINKING UP SIGNS AND DOING THEIR HAIR.

JORDAN
PENETRATED WITH
AUTHORITY.

this is how well a ballclub plays over the course of a season. You know, you make this record run or whatever you're trying to do to try to establish a homecourt advantage. And you get enamored with just winning games, and winning games. But then there's another level that comes at the end of the season. Playoff basket-ball totally changes everything. That's the mystery, as to whether we can play at this level all through the season and then come through with a championship drive."

In other words, Jackson was worried that his team would get so drunk with winning during the regular season that they wouldn't play sharp ball in the playoffs. If necessary, Jackson planned to slow them down. But he acknowledged a potential danger.

"You can actually take them out of their rhythm by resting guys in a different rotation off the bench," Jackson explained. "I have considered that."

Such talk from the coach only seemed to drive the Bulls harder to keep winning. "What amazes me most about our team," Jack Haley said after the Charlotte game, "is that we probably have the league's greatest player ever in Michael Jordan, we have the league's greatest rebounder in Dennis Rodman, and

we have what is probably this year's MVP in Scottie Pippen, and what amazes me most is the work ethic and leadership that these three guys bring to the floor night in and night out. With all of the accolades, with all of the money, with all of the championships, everything that they have, what motivates them besides

winning another championship? How many months away is that? And these guys are focused now."

Jackson suggested that one big part of the season's mystery would be Rodman's continuing adjustment to the Bulls. "We're all waiting for the other shoe to drop with Dennis, so to speak," the coach said in January.

KUKOC HIMSELF TOOK FLIGHT TO THE RIM IN A WIN OVER HOUSTON.

ANY BULL WHO HAD AN EYE FOR A
REBOUND USUALLY HAD TO FIGHT
RODMAN FOR IT.

THE SPOTLIGHT ALSO FELL ON THE SUBS, TOO, INCLUDING WENNINGTON.

IS THAT JUD BUECHLER OR BILL RUSSELL?

"At least the media are kind of looking for that. We're just saying, 'Everything's going good. Just pay attention to basketball and do what comes natural, and that's play and enjoy the game.' "

It was obvious that Rodman loved being in Chicago and loved playing for Jackson. Most of all he loved playing with Jordan and Pippen, who worked extremely hard in practice, something that Rodman felt that David Robinson never understood.

Rodman's meshing on the court led to a thaw of relationships off it. "With Jordan and Pippen, you're talking about two superstars who were not at all threatened by Dennis," Jack Haley said. "They did-

n't care about his hair color. They don't care about anything. If the man gets 20 rebounds a game and we win, that's all they care about. What he does off the floor, they couldn't care less about that or anything else, as long as he comes to work. And that's what Dennis is about. 'Leave me alone. Let me have my outside life. Let me come do my job as a player. Let my actions on the floor speak for me.' The Bulls have been tremendous for Dennis. Again, everyone just gave him his space, and he just kind of slowly opened up."

Certainly the professional atmosphere around the Bulls was good for Rodman. It also didn't hurt that he was in the last year of his contract and badly in need of another. The

Bulls hoped that that, as much as anything, would keep him vigilant.

Yet contrary to Haley's assertions, the other shoe did fall just three nights after his vote of confidence. After the win in Charlotte, the Bulls returned to the United Center and easily dismissed the Milwaukee Bucks, then turned their attention to a much-anticipated rematch with the SuperSonics, who with a 23-10 record were second in the league behind Chicago's 28-3.

Seattle had been limiting teams to just 97 points per game, but the Bulls shot nearly 60 percent while clamping down on defense. In the first half, Rodman got into a woofing match with Sonics backup Frank Brickowski. But the real trouble

JORDAN AND COMPANY DUSTED THE SONICS IN JANUARY.

came in the last minute of the third period when Rodman was whistled for fouling Shawn Kemp, then argued with official Terry Durham. Longley stepped in to restrain his teammate, but official Ron Olesiak hit Rodman with a second technical foul.

It was the first time Rodman was

tossed from a game since the previous April when he played for San Antonio.

As for the outcome, his absence really didn't matter. The Bulls had already made their run and cruised in the fourth period to a 113-87 win. And Haley assured everyone who would listen that Rodman

would continue to produce outstanding basketball, control his emotions as best such a free spirit ever could – and meanwhile, try to be one of the fellas. In his own way, of course.

"What's been really good here is that Michael Jordan and I and Scottie Pippen and I are very good

Nathaniel S. Butler/NBA photo

friends," Haley said. "We play a lot of cards together, and we do a lot of stuff off the floor. Dennis has been kind of put in a position, where, if we're on the road or something and he wants to go to dinner or he wants to do something with me, and I'm going out with the other guys, then he's kind of forced to come along.

He's been put in a situation where, 'Sit in my room and be alone,' or 'Go hang out with my best friend, Jack, who is consequently with Michael and Scottie.'

"Since he has respect for these guys, and since they don't really care, they've gotten through," Haley added. "Michael and Dennis are

doing great. Scottie and Dennis still have no conversation really other than basketball. Scottie and Dennis tremendously respect each other, but I don't see those two going to dinner too often. I think that goes back to the Piston days, I really do. They'll always play together and be phenomenal teammates, but when they walk

RODMAN WOULD FIGHT A WHOLE TEAM FOR A REBOUND, AND THIS TIME AGAINST THE KNICKS, HE HAD NO CHOICE.

Scott Cunningham/NBA photo

AT THE END OF JANUARY, THE BULLS WENT TO HOUSTON AND WON THEIR FIRST GAME THERE IN YEARS.

off the floor and it's time to go hang out...no. But Dennis has warmed to this team. For example, two nights ago Steve Kerr, Jud Buechler, Luc Longley, myself and Toni Kukoc all went out. Dennis again had to come along. Once he got out with the guys, he opened up and picked up the tab.

"These guys were stunned because here we are, midway through the season, and he's out with the guys having a good time."

The next stop on the schedule was Philadelphia, where 76ers rookie Jerry Stackhouse, who had drawn comparisons with Jordan because of his elevated game and University of

North Carolina background, had been quoted in the newspapers as saying that "nobody can stop me in this league – not even Michael Jordan."

Jordan's reply was 48 points while Stackhouse finished the night with nine. The two had a running conversation throughout the game, during

which Jordan repeatedly told Stackhouse to settle down.

"It was just very clinical," observed Philly great Julius Erving, who was in the audience.

Indeed, that could describe the Bulls' performance for the month. They rolled to 14 straight wins, their first undefeated month in team history.

The next contest, a Martin Luther King day matinee in Washington, brought yet another 46-point performance from Jordan, including 19 points in the fourth quarter that were needed to fell the Bullets, 116-109, in a late comeback.

After the victory over Washington, Jackson was asked again –very pointedly – about the possibility of a 70-win season, and he replied that there were so many difficult points to any year, he didn't really consider the magic 70 as a reality.

The Bulls seemed to take their coach's assessment as another challenge. They kept churning out victories through the winter of 1996. The

Washington win was followed by another close road victory over the Toronto Raptors. Jordan had 38 and another 15 in the fourth quarter.

After two days rest, the Bulls faced the surging Pistons, coached by former Bulls coach Doug Collins, at the United Center in a nationally televised game. Jordan scored 36 and Pippen 22 to settle the matter early and send their old coach a message, 111-96.

For their 35th win, the Bulls moved to New York and humiliated a reeling Knicks team, 99-79, in Madison Square Garden, where rumors swirled that new coach Don Nelson was about to be fired. "I can't remember the last time we blew out this team in this building," Jordan said.

From there, the Bulls went home to record three more wins over Vancouver, Miami and Phoenix, hiking their record to 38-3. "I think a lot of teams are very afraid of the Chicago Bulls," Rodman said, "just because of who the individuals are,

just because they have to concentrate on so many people. A lot of teams are really skeptical. They're saying, 'What are we gonna do now?'"

They closed a perfect month with a perfect win, a road victory over Houston in the Summit, the first time the Bulls had won there in eight years. "We had a little meeting after our morning shootaround and I told the guys that personally I don't think I've come out of this building with a win as a head coach," Jackson said.

"I don't think we've won here since Ralph Sampson played here," added Pippen, whose 28 points keyed Chicago's 98-87 victory. "That's been quite some time."

Asked what it felt like to defeat the defending world champions, Rodman said, "They're not the world champions right now. They're just the Houston Rockets. They're a good team, but we'll find out who the champs are in June."

JACKSON CAUTIONED HIS PLAYERS TO DEAL WITH THEIR SUCCESS MODESTLY.

YET THE OFFICIALS COULD STILL DRAW HIS IRE EVERY NOW AND THEN.

IT WAS THE GRIND, THE TREADMILL, JACKSON SAID, THAT GOT TO MOST NBA COACHES.

JACKSON AND HIS STAFF WERE DETERMINED TO DRILL HIS PLAYERS IN THE FUNDAMENTALS, AN APPROACH THAT JORDAN AND PIPPEN EMBRACED.

"Somewhere about the middle of training camp, I realized I was having a lot of fun coaching this team, and Dennis Rodman to me brings a lot of levity to the game," Jackson explained. "I mean, I get a kick out of watching him play."

Most important, though, Jackson did a dipstick check on his own intensity levels. The season opened with the NBA's regular officials on strike, which meant the league had put together two-man replacement crews from the Continental Basketball Association. Jackson always had expended a good deal of energy each game riding the refs, but dealing with the replacements' unorthodox calls brought him to a new revelation.

"I realized that it didn't matter what referees do out there, there's not much you can do walking up and down the court and yelling," he said. "I decided I was going to have to sit down and shut up and enjoy the game and coach at the timeouts and coach at the practices rather than on the floor, and practice what I preached a little bit."

The unspoken truth here was that the coaches couldn't expect Rodman to behave better if they weren't doing the same. Jackson still had his moments of animation – especially when Toni Kukoc took an ill-advised three-point try – but he turned his demeanor down yet another notch, much to the delight of his players.

Asked about Jackson early in the year, Rodman said, "Well, he's laid back. He's a Deadhead." Rodman laughed hard at this assessment, and when a reporter asked, "Is he your kind of coach?" Dennis replied, "Oh yeah. He's fancy free, don't give a damn. With him, it's just, 'Go out there and do the job, and let's go home and have a cold one.' "

Later in the season, when John Salley was added to the roster, he gained an immediate appreciation for Jackson's style. "A lot of coaches on other teams get mad that Phil just sits there," Salley said. "It makes them look bad. But he sits there because that's his seat. He prepares us enough in practice, trust me, that he doesn't have to do all that whooping and hollering, all those sideline antics. A lot of coaches get into that yelling and whooping and hollering, carrying on and trying to demean a guy. They say, 'Well I'm trying to get them to play harder.' Well, no, some coaches are just angry, frustrated fans."

The results, perhaps, provide the greatest testimonial. The 1995-96 season marked Jackson's seventh consecutive campaign coaching the Bulls, the longest tenure in one job among the NBA's 29 coaches, and during that time he guided his club to four championships. He accomplished those things by overcoming the elements that had made casualties of many of his peers – the exhausting grind of the 82-game schedule, the daily practices, the shuffling and reshuffling of priorities, and always the pressure to win.

Jackson's simple answer had been to find his sense of self elsewhere. "Sometimes, I think you have to jump off the treadmill," he said. "Step back a little ways from it, relook it and rethink it."

If that meant preaching to his players about the great white buffalo or giving them obscure books to read or having them pause amid the looniness of the NBA for a meditation session, so be it. On more than

JIM CLEAMONS, JACKSON, JIMMY RODGERS, AND TEX WINTER, FOUR OF THE BULLS FIVE COACHES. JOHN PAXSON, NOT PICTURED, OFTEN DID THE TEAM'S ADVANCE SCOUTING REPORTS.

one occasion, Jackson's approach has left his players shaking their heads in amusement. "He's our guru," Michael Jordan said when asked about Jackson's quirkiness in early 1996. "He's got that yen, that Zen stuff, working in our favor."

But make no mistake, Jackson is so compelling a figure that, while his players may not accept each and every one of his unconventional remedies, they showed an utter and complete faith in him. And they understood when Jackson spoke of the spiritual connection to the game. Jordan credited just that connection with showing him how to relate to less-talented teammates.

"I think Phil really has given me a chance to be patient and taught me how to understand the supporting cast of teammates and give them a chance to improve," Jordan said.

"He's an interesting guy," Steve Kerr said of Jackson. "He keeps things very refreshing for us all season. He keeps things fun. He never loses sight of the fact that basketball is a game. It's supposed to be fun. He doesn't let us forget about that. But at the same time, this is our job, too, and he doesn't let us forget about that, either."

That's not to say that Jackson would hesitate to get in a player's face, Kerr added. "But when he does

it," Kerr said, "you know it's not personal. That's his strength. He always maintains authority without being a dictator. And he always maintains his friendship without kissing up. He just finds that perfect balance, and because of that he always has everybody's respect. And ultimately the hardest part of being a coach in the NBA, I think, is having every player's respect."

Jackson knows the faith his players have in him is no small thing. "I believe that there is a tenuous trial sometimes between coaches and

players," he says. "I've found that I have the confidence of my group, so that they feel comfortable. And it's not anything where if I try experimental things that they feel threatened or can't deal with it. It's sort of something where I've had an open

STEVE KERR SAID THAT HAVING THE RESPECT OF THE PLAYERS WAS JACKSON'S GREAT SUCCESS.

HE KEPT THEM FOCUSED ON THE TEAM IDENTITY.

JUD BUECHLER LOOKING FOR THE OPEN MAN.

EVERYONE KNEW RODMAN COULD GET INTO THE AIR, BUT SITTING IN THE PILOT'S SEAT ON THE TEAM PLANE MIGHT HAVE BEEN A BIT MUCH.

working forum to try a variety of styles and approaches, all of which seem to be enjoyable to them. The only thing they don't like is monotony and constancy. But we still make one thing constant, and that's fundamentals. The one thing that we always strive for is to make fundamentals and execution a part of our game."

The dedication of the Bulls' coaching staff to fundamentals had always been paramount, and it was matched by Jordan's and Pippen's commitment each and every practice to working at positioning, dribbling, passing, shooting, footwork, the elements that many pro players neglect from their earliest days in the game.

In fact, the Bulls' remarkable success in 1996 was a testament to their dedication to fundamentals and to the absence of them on other teams. Quite often, Jordan and Pippen would prey on the poor passing of younger, unschooled opponents, and afterward the Bulls coaching staff would smile knowingly.

February opened with the Bulls headed out of Houston with a win

and moving full-speed ahead on their second western road trip. That's when the trouble that Jackson had forecast finally arrived.

Longley went on the injured list with a sprained knee just before a Chicago victory in Sacramento. Then, against the Kings, Kukoc rolled over an ankle, just as he was starting to find a comfort zone coming off the bench.

"We were hitting a low point right before we left on the road trip," Jackson explained. "Scottie sprained an arch. Luc had knee problems; he couldn't practice. Dennis dislocated a finger; he was out. So we missed some key practices right before we went away. As a consequence, I could see us disintegrating a little bit. We had a 20-turnover game and we were shooting only 45 percent. Suddenly, we weren't as hot as we were before."

Despite the Bulls' problems, they whipped the Kings by 20, then headed to Los Angeles for a game the next night against the Lakers, who had just welcomed Magic Johnson back from retirement. Despite being substantially heavier than during his glory days, Johnson had played well his first game back against Golden State, which meant that anticipation was high for this

rematch with Jordan. At one point, a delirious fan ran onto the Forum floor and clutched a startled and somewhat frightened Jordan around the legs before the fellow was led away by security.

The Bulls put aside the distractions and easily outclassed the Lakers.

"I hope Magic's comeback is as effective as Michael's, but I still have my doubts," Jackson said later. "I watched him play out there in L.A. I saw a guy with 30 pounds more on his body, and I don't know. I know what Michael went through to get back and to suddenly put yourself in that grind physically, to get beat up, your knees, your ankles, your body's bruised. It's a process."

After a Saturday night off, the Bulls headed to Denver, where Mahmoud Abdul-Rauf lay waiting with his quick-release jumper. The Nuggets buried the Bulls in a 31-point first half lead, but Jordan shook off a three-game slump, scoring 39 points and driving Chicago back, right to the edge of winning. Denver held on, though, to hand the Bulls just their fourth loss.

Two nights later, the Bulls lost a second consecutive game for the first time all season when Charles Barkley powered Phoenix with 35 points and

THE BULLS CAME AND WENT AT THEIR HOTELS LIKE ROCK STARS.

CAFFEY IN A QUIET PRE-GAME MOMENT AT THE GREAT WESTERN FORUM.

16 rebounds. The loss had a familiar, disturbing pattern in that the Bulls fell far behind early, then stormed back, only to lose late.

"Two good opponents were ready for us, and they both got us," Jackson said. "We made great comebacks. We didn't get the lead against Phoenix, but we tied it a couple of times down the stretch. It's obvious that Michael has his nights. He missed a couple of free throws in Phoenix that could have given us the lead and maybe won the ballgame for us. It's never his effort or his competitive drive that you worry about. It's never that he's coming to the game and something's not going to happen because of the way he plays. He's going to find a way to make his team competitive by the way he plays. If it's not his shooting, it's his passing or rebounding or whatever. That's the knack that older players like Michael and Magic have for lifting the level of their teams."

This "knack" saved the Bulls from a third straight loss when they traveled to Golden State and again fell behind. Jordan fueled another comeback, but this time he insisted on finishing with a win, even though it meant that he had to play long minutes to get it. Jackson said, "In the second half, I said to Michael, 'Do you want to come out now?' He said, 'No.' I said, 'If you don't come out now, you're gonna go all the way.' He said, 'Then I'll have to go all the way then.'

"Somewhere in the fourth quarter, I called two timeouts basically for Michael, just to get him some rest because his knees were killing him. So after the game we sat down. I said, 'What'd you play, 46 minutes?' In the old days, he could play a 46-minute game. I said, 'Good, we tried it out. We saw how far you could go. But I think a 42-minute game is probably the duration that you have to look at.'

"That tells me something about Michael Jordan," Jackson said. "In the old days, he could play a 58-minute game and still be going strong at the end of it. His feet are made of clay, and he's starting to get older."

The game against the Warriors also marked the Bulls' reunion with former teammate B.J. Armstrong, who, rather than expressing bitterness over being traded, chose to rely on the class he had always shown in Chicago. "I won three champi-

onships in six years," Armstrong told reporters. "I can't ask for more. I feel fortunate."

Their two losses on the western trip left the Bulls at 42-5 heading into the All-Star break, where the main news was that Rodman had not been selected with Jordan, Pippen and Jackson. In an amazing year, Rodman had managed to swing his life around, from his troubles in Texas to his seeming triumph in Chicago. As February neared, he had become anxious about making the All-Star team.

The 1996 All-Star weekend was going to be held in San Antonio, which would have made Rodman's appearance very satisfying, indeed. Although he was high in the fan voting, Dennis didn't have enough votes to earn a starting slot, so he would have to depend on the vote of the Eastern Conference's coaches to be named as a reserve.

"We're looking forward to that," Haley said. "We're hoping and praying he makes the team so he can go back to San Antonio and say, 'Hey, look at me now.' "

THE BULLS BUMPED MAGIC AROUND AND WELCOMED HIM BACK TO THE LEAGUE.

A GOOD HUMORED MOMENT BETWEEN MAGIC AND MICHAEL.

SECURITY HAD TO CONTROL THIS EMOTIONAL FAN WHO CAME AFTER JORDAN IN LOS ANGELES.

MICHAEL WENT TO GREAT LENGTHS TO FIND SOME SOLITUDE AWAY FROM THE PRESS BEFORE GAMES, AND THE TEAM PLANE WAS A SANCTUARY.

The coaches, however, overlooked Rodman for the fourth straight year, despite the fact that he was clearly on his way to winning a fifth straight league rebounding title. On his Chicago radio show, Rodman angrily lashed out that the coaches had engaged in a conspiracy to keep him out of the game. Depressed, he went to Vegas and vacationed while the rest of the NBA's elite players headed to Texas and basked in the limelight that Rodman craved.

Without Rodman's technicolor revue, the highlights of All-Star Weekend were more subtle. For example, the format forced Jackson to hold his first open practice in years. There, all-stars from other teams were required to go through the fundamental drills that characterize every Bulls' practice. Milwaukee's Vin Baker noted that Jackson had him doing things he hadn't done since junior high. Then Jackson introduced the players to some triple-post offensive spacing that left several all-stars moving cautiously around the court, unsure of exactly where they were supposed to be.

During the first brief scrimmage, Miami's Alonzo Mourning was left on the sideline with Charlotte's Glen Rice. It was perhaps the first time in years, probably since grade school, that Mourning hadn't been chosen

first for side, and he stood courtside with his arms folded, his face growing redder by the minute as Jackson's chosen first two units practiced.

Finally Mourning nudged Jackson and said, "How 'bout putting me in?"

"I will in a minute," Jackson said. "There's just a few more things I want to see."

You had to wonder, with the playoffs looming just eight weeks ahead, if Jackson wasn't already playing mind games with an opponent. The All-Star game itself generated similar thoughts. Jordan had staked the East stars to a big lead, and then Jackson benched him midway through the second half to allow Shaquille O'Neal, who had grown up in San Antonio, to run up big numbers on a series of thunder dunks and crowd-pleasing plays.

But it was obvious that Jordan was the most valuable player, and when the media voted him so after the game, the local partisans in the Alamodome booed.

Jordan was a bit taken aback by the whole display and even offered to give O'Neal the trophy. The real point, however, was that Jackson had favored the Orlando center over his own star, thus making sure not to give Shaq any emotional ammunition for later in the season against the Bulls. And just to make sure the

JAMES EDWARDS CAME OFF THE INJURED LIST TO PROVIDE SOME OFFENSE ON THE WESTERN ROAD TRIP. UNFORTUNATELY, HE COULDN'T GET THE BULLS OVER THE HUMP AGAINST DENVER.

atmosphere stayed light, Jordan snuck up and pulled down the warm-up pants of Orlando's Anfernee Hardaway just as he stepped up for his pregame introduc-

DENVER AND PHOENIX HANDED THE BULLS THEIR FIRST BACK-TO-BACK LOSSES OF THE SEASON IN EARLY FEBRUARY.

AT THE END OF THE ROAD TRIP, JACKSON PACKED UP AND HEADED TO THE ALL STAR GAME.

THE WARRIORS WOULD HAVE MADE IT THREE STRAIGHT LOSSES IF MICHAEL HADN'T BEEN DETERMINED TO PLAY LONG MINUTES TO GET THE WIN.

tion. The message was clear for the young Magic stars: It was hard not to like these Chicago guys.

During the All-Star festivities, Jackson said much of the Bulls' success would be determined by how their Eastern Conference opponents adjusted to them over the second half of the season.

"We're waiting," he said, "to see how things go the third and fourth time we play teams, and then we'll feel like, 'Yes, the other teams aren't making the adjustments, or we're making the adjustments ahead of them.' That will tell us how we're going to do in the playoffs when it

gets to be a seven-game series."

Jackson got his first indication right after the break, as Chicago raced out to six straight wins. Jordan scored 32 to dump the Bullets in the United Center.

Then came a satisfying overtime triumph over the Pistons in Detroit. The Bulls had led by 11 with seven minutes to play, then fell asleep at the wheel and watched the Pistons take a five-point margin with 37.7 seconds left.

But Kukoc hit a clutch three, and Rodman, who finished with 19 rebounds – including a season-high 14 on the offensive glass –hit a last-second stickback to tie it. From there, Jordan scored eight in overtime to notch the 44th win.

Next they got a close win in Minneapolis, then dipped down to Indianapolis where Jordan scored 44 points, Pippen 40 and Rodman fought his way to 23 rebounds to beat the Pacers, 110-104.

"They're the best," Pacers coach Larry Brown said, shaking his head. "They wouldn't be 46-5 if they didn't try to make a statement every game."

The next declaration came with an exclamation point in the United Center, 102-76 over Cleveland, as the Bulls got 22 points from Ron Harper, the former Cavalier.

From there, the Bulls jetted south for a close win at Atlanta before getting scorched by Rex Chapman and Miami. The Heat had just eight players available after a late trade, but that's all Pat Riley's team needed. "We played hard, and Rex reminded me of Jerry West," Riley said, smiling. In fact, Chapman scored 39 points by mailing in a host of threes.

What the season's sixth loss turned out to be was just the right wake-up call for the Bulls' next test, against Orlando in the United Center. Kukoc scored 24 points in 23 minutes, including 11 in a row to start the fourth period, that had the Bulls bench, Jordan included, up and dancing.

The Magic fell, 111-91, and looked quite glum afterward.

"MJ and Pip had been carrying us for so long, so I needed to do something," said Toni, who hit six of eight three-point attempts.

The next night, the Bulls blew past Minnesota to gain their 50th win, making them the quickest team in league history to tally that number. Jordan had 35 points, Kukoc 23, and Rodman pulled in another 24 rebounds. The biggest news seemed to be that the Croatian had finally learned to contribute off the bench. His confidence had re-emerged, and it was none too soon, because things were about to get crazy.

NO MATTER HOW BIG, RODMAN WAS WILLING TO CHALLENGE ALL TAKERS.

A LATE FEBRUARY WIN OVER ORLANDO WAS ANOTHER CONFIDENCE BOOSTER.

7

STARTING WITH TRAINING CAMP, when he found out that he would lose his place in the Bulls starting lineup to Dennis Rodman, the season had been one long painful adjustment for Toni Kukoc.

It had been Phil Jackson's hope that Kukoc would embrace the sixth-man role and find a comfort level, giving the Bulls an offensive punch off the bench. After all, his 6-11 height and unique ballhandling and passing skills made Kukoc an impossible matchup for many teams. Plus, he had long arms and spidery post moves that sometimes brought to mind former Boston Celtic great Kevin McHale.

"I talked to him both about John Havlicek and Kevin McHale," Jackson said, "how they're both in the Hall of Fame (McHale surely will be elected on the first ballot) and they were both sixth men for a major part of their careers."

Kukoc's response had been to point out that the post wasn't his natural game, despite his height. "Actually I never played as a post-up player before I came here," he said. "I know a few moves that I used playing down low in Europe, but it's forced a little bit."

Kukoc played well in spots over the first half of the season, but the consistency of his performances remained a major problem. It was on defense that Kukoc struggled most. The coaches found that he had trouble with stronger players in the low post, and that quicker guards could get past him on the perimeter to break down the Bulls' defense.

These circumstances weren't uncommon for other versatile young players in the NBA, but Kukoc's background as a star in the European leagues created higher expectations for the 26-year-old Croatian. He wanted to be as successful in America as he had been in Europe.

"Toni is real conscious of his abilities and very cognizant of the fact that he wants to be an all-star and wants to prove his worth," Jackson said at midseason. "He feels like he's not having an ample opportunity to contribute to our victories because so many of them have been runaways. He hasn't felt like he's really had an opportunity to get a vital role for the team, to where they need him, and I think he likes to be needed.

KUKOC AND LONGLEY GAVE THE BULLS A GLOBAL GAME.

"He gets down on himself, and we have to encourage him not to feel down. He's very unusual, not the kind of player we're used to here in the United States. A lot of players would be very used to you yelling at them or kicking their butt. But Toni responds much differently than that. He's more of a pat-on-the-back kind of guy. He's a guy who responds more to concrete criticism done at a very low-key level postgame."

"I'm not handling it well," Kukoc admitted. "It's hard. I'm not used to it. Sometimes I feel cold on the bench. I'm trying to find ways to stay warm and focused, but it's just not there. I've tried everything: working out right before a game to stay warm, lying down instead of sitting, stretching."

One writer suggested, tongue in cheek, that he look into practicing some of Jackson's Zen. "I'm not going to try that," Kukoc said, hinting playfully at his differences with the coach.

Yet at times, Jordan and Pippen rode Kukoc every bit as hard as Jackson. Much of it was pointed criticism aimed at bringing his style of play in line with the physical NBA game. Some of it was just talk. When Kukoc put on a pair of Jordan's patent-leather Nikes for a game one night, Jordan eyed him and said, "Don't embarrass my shoes."

Jackson's main complaint was that Kukoc sometimes took a three-pointer at the wrong moment in games, when a miss could give the opponent unnecessary momentum. "I talked to Toni about how important it is for him to score to feel a part of the game," Jackson said.

WENNINGTON FOUND THE BULLS TO BE ONE OF LIFE'S GREAT RIDES.

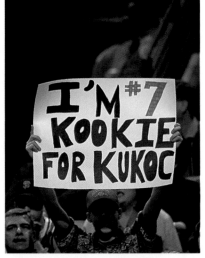

JACKSON AND KUKOC DIDN'T ALWAYS AGREE, BUT THE CROATIAN STAR EVENTUALLY FOUND SOME COMFORT AS THE SIXTH MAN.

"And I tried to get him a scoring slot right away to get him feeling like he was a part of it.

"One of the games I got on Toni a little was right before we went on the road trip in early February. Against Phoenix, he threw up a three-pointer when we had a better option right in front of him and he could have made the pass. He said basically it was his fifth or sixth trip down the floor and he hadn't really taken a shot yet, and he felt the need to. So we talked a little bit about getting into the game by getting a good shot. So I think he's been conscious of that. He might have done it at an inappropriate moment. Still, I think that we understand his psyche, and it's alright.

"I told him, 'Go ahead, be my guest, as long as it's not in the fourth quarter at a critical point in the game. We'll get something accomplished early in the game so you feel a part of it, if that's what it takes to get you going.'

"I think he's shown that he can really contribute for us," Jackson added. "In big games, he plays big, and we're real comfortable with what he can do."

Kukoc was one of three international athletes among the Bulls' top eight players, the other two being Longley, an Australian, and Wennington, a Canadian. Kukoc, a Croatian who had been groomed since childhood for Yugoslavia's national teams, was the only one of the three who had not played college hoops in the United States. While Kukoc's adjustment was clearly the toughest, Longley's was far from problem-free. After all, he was the starting center.

"We felt from the beginning that if we were going to win the championship, Luc was going to have to do the job for us," explained Tex Winter, an indicating of the pressure Longley faced.

"To be perfectly honest," Winter added, "there's been times he's done the job, but there's been an awful lot of times where he's disappointed not

only us but himself. And we don't know where we stand as we get near the playoffs with him, because he has not shown up to the extent that we had hoped he would. Defensively, his job has been fairly good. He takes up a lot of space. His presence out there is a factor, but maybe not

the factor we think it could be. Offense is where he has struggled, really. He does some things nicely. He passes the ball well, but he just has a tough time scoring, putting the ball in the basket, even on easy shots sometimes."

Actually, Longley possessed a nice

KUKOC HAD HIS OWN WAY OF PRESENTING MATCHUP PROBLEMS.

Barry Gossage/NBA photo

TEX WINTER LIKED TO SEE LUC FINISH WITH AUTHORITY.

face-up jumper from 10 to 15 feet, but it was around the basket that his finishing skills left Winter so exasperated. Like Kukoc, Longley also took a regular scalding from Jordan and Pippen. Scottie, in particular, did not like to see the big Aussie give up position easily on defense.

Still, all parties involved admitted that Longley had made big progress since coming to the Bulls. "He's plugging the lane and putting his body on guys going to the basket," Jackson had said in February. "I think he's doing a great job when guys go to the basket, and he just steps over and seals the lane. Those are things that a big guy who wants to cover the lane can do."

"It's my most important focus on the team," Longley said of his defensive role, adding that Rodman's presence had speeded up his process of maturity. "Dennis certainly helps a lot because you can commit to being a defensive presence, you can commit to the ball because you know he's going to drop in behind you and cover your backside."

Longley also knew that his continued defensive improvement was going to be a key for the playoffs because of the challenge he would face from the Eastern Conference's best centers — Shaquille O'Neal, Patrick Ewing and Alonzo Mourning. Facing them would be a final exam for his season, he said.

To answer Longley's critics, Jackson liked to point out that the Bulls just weren't as good whenever the center was out with an injury. "Luc's real important to us because he's got that body size that helps us out defensively," Jackson said. "He sets picks. When he's been out, we miss his size. It frees up guys for open shots and gives Dennis a lot of room in the middle and helps our defense out.

"As far as his offensive prowess goes, I don't know if Luc's ever going to have the offensive skills necessary to be a big offensive player in this game. But what impresses us is that our offense is based around a sideline triangle. He's the apex of that triangle. We need to get the ball inside, and he passes the ball extremely well. He's an unselfish kid, and that's more important than anything else.

"Then, his attitude. He's a real good team man. He's a mate, as he always calls himself, a good mate. From that standpoint, he's fit in real well in the chemistry of our team."

The turn that Toni Kukoc was waiting for came much sooner than he expected. Through February, the team watched as Scottie Pippen's MVP season fell victim to pain in his back, legs and ankles. The wear and tear had produced new injuries and inflamed old ones.

The smile that had inhabited his face prior to the All-Star game was replaced by a grimace. He tried shoe lifts and a variety of other remedies. "I even changed my hairdo a little bit," he joked.

The circumstances, however, began to generate some conflict within the organization. Management and the coaching staff wanted Pippen to take some time off to get healthy for the playoffs, but he was insistent that he keep playing.

While the debate rolled into March, the Bulls just kept winning, pushing their record to 51-6 with a 110-87 home win over Golden State and B.J. Armstrong on the first day of the month.

WENNINGTON HAD HIS OWN TAKE ON THE BULLS' GREAT RUN.

"What a difference a year makes," noted Chicago Tribune beat writer Terry Armour. "A year ago Michael Jordan was with the White Sox in spring training in Sarasota, Florida, B.J. Armstrong was wearing a Bulls uniform, and the Bulls were flirting with mediocrity with a 28-29 record."

The next evening brought another blowout over the Celtics and more worries, as Rodman continued his long-running dispute with official Terry Durham. "I've been having problems with him since I've been in

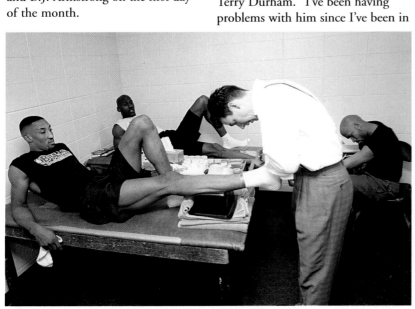

TRAINER CHIP SCHAEFER WORKED ON PIPPEN'S TROUBLESOME ANKLES.

LONGLEY HAD THE SIZE THE BULLS NEEDED.

JORDAN
DISCOVERED THAT
THE SEASON WAS
THE VERY BEST OF
TIMES.

the league," Rodman said.

Three nights later, Rodman was ejected for a flagrant foul in the third period of a home win over Milwaukee. "That was a bad call," Jackson said.

The next victim was Detroit, 102-81, and Jordan led the way with a season-high 53 points, which left Doug Collins shaking his head. "Michael is so tenacious," he said, "and he knows when to go for it."

Floating on this euphoria, the

Bulls traveled to New York and promptly got their balloons popped by a Knicks team rebounding from the firing of coach Don Nelson and the promotion of former assistant Jeff Van Gundy. The 104-72 blowout was the worst loss of the season.

The worst news was that Pippen had reinjured his ankle, intensifying the debate over whether he should take a break. "He's had a few nagging injuries he cannot shake," Jordan said. "What's important is

that we rally around him. He has to take care of himself physically. If it means playing less, sitting, it's a judgment he has to make. Seventy wins is something we shouldn't worry about. We want to be healthy down the stretch."

The comment from Jordan was substantial because he, too, had battled management over injury his second year in the league, returning for the 1986 playoffs against Reinsdorf's and Krause's wishes. The principle

FACING THE BULLS WAS ENOUGH TO BRING A GULP FROM OPPONENTS.

established then was that an athlete knows his body better than anyone else. But the team had a lot at stake now, and Jordan was advising Pippen, who was determined to see the Bulls win 70, to sit.

That Wednesday, March 13, team doctors examined Pippen and determined there was no sign of a disk problem in his back. His knees, however, were getting worse. With that news, Pippen agreed to take up to 10 days off.

At first, Jackson thought about moving Steve Kerr into the starting lineup, but finally he decided to go with Kukoc. "Scottie brings the element of speed and quickness to our defense," Jackson said. "We hope Toni can pick up the slack."

That night Kukoc scored 16 to go with Jordan's 37 and Longley's 16 in a home blowout of Washington. Two nights later, Kukoc hit for 24 to go with Jordan's 33 in a romp over visit-

ing Denver.

The big moment, however, came before the game when Nugget guard Mahmoud Abdul-Rauf agreed to stand for the National Anthem, breaking the season-long silent protest that had generated international attention.

Unfortunately, Rodman grabbed the spotlight away from Abdul-Rauf the next night by getting ejected during a road win over New Jersey. He was called for a foul in the first period, then put his hands in his pants, an apparent sign of protest, which brought another whistle from official Ted Bernhardt. Furious, Rodman rushed up to Bernhardt and head-butted him, then threw a tirade before leaving the court, turning over a drink container and rearranging some courtside furniture.

"It was an accidental head butt," the Worm maintained afterward.

Then he said, "I'm picked on

KRAUSE SIGNED SALLEY AS A FREE AGENT IN MARCH.

THE WORM SHOWED THE PISTONS HIS OFFENSIVE STYLE.

every game. I'm gonna be a guinea pig for everything on the court. Why am I so different than the rest of the league? They're gonna suspend me no matter. Suspend me, suspend me. I don't care. Make an example out of Dennis Rodman."

The league fined him $20,000 and suspended him six games, costing Rodman nearly another $200,000 in lost salary. Suddenly, the radio talk shows had forgotten

Abdul-Rauf and were turning their attention to the dyed man.

Sitting courtside, Jackson had responded with a wry smile during the blowup. But the incident left the Bulls angry and just a bit worried. Jordan was furious that Rodman had picked the very day that Pippen began his recovery.

With the team's leading rebounders out, Jordan responded with 16 boards and 37 points to whip New

Jersey.

Given a little time to think about it, Rodman was contrite the next morning and even took the unusual step of phoning Jordan to ask a routine question. It was the Worm's way of apologizing, his teammates figured. But the clouds of doubt had already gathered.

"We're trying to progress as a team, and he kind of let it go by the wayside," Jordan said. "A lot of what

you see in Dennis is his image and persona. He has continued to feed off that. That's very dangerous to this team's success."

Yet this was the kind of season where the Bulls could turn even setbacks into blessings. Rodman's suspension and Pippen's injury gave Kukoc the playing time to find some comfort level. He scored 21 points with 11 assists and six rebounds to complement Jordan's 38 points and

11 rebounds in a four-point win over Philadelphia two nights later. It was Jackson's 400th coaching victory, and Jordan played 47 minutes to earn it.

The Bulls returned home to whip Sacramento, and Rodman issued an apology to the entire team. On the very day he was suspended, a city clothier, Bigsby and Kruthers, had just put the finishing touches on his likeness on one of its billboards alongside the Kennedy Expressway.

But the sight of Rodman in a suit was just too great an inconsistency for Chicago commuters, causing many drivers to slow down for a double take.

The ensuing traffic tie-ups were dangerous, police said, and the situation forced the clothier to paint over the likeness within a matter of days. It seemed that Rodman was finding conflict with authority at every turn.

Yet there was no question that the

BUT DETROIT WAS MORE WORRIED ABOUT JORDAN.

Scott Cunningham/NBA photo

RODMAN'S INCREASED IRRITATION WITH OFFICIALS LED TO HIS BLOWUP, BUT THE FANS LET IT BE KNOWN WHERE THEY STOOD.

city's infatuation had grown. Unable to wear the number 10 he had worn most of his career because it was the retired number of Bulls great Bob Love, Rodman had gained permission from the league to wear number 91, because 9 and 1 added up to 10. Rodman's practice of removing his jersey and giving it to a fan each night as he left the United Center floor soon created a flurry of fan interest, and number 91s became hot items.

Each night the arena was dotted with sign-toting fans eager to get Rodman's attention and jersey. "People are offering their sisters," quipped the Worm, who had given the members of the Red Hot Chili Peppers a jersey. The band, in turn, wore No. 91s on stage during their concert.

During Rodman's suspension, one fan held up a sign that read, "Hey, Rodman, mail me your jersey." Later, upon his return, another patron took the direct approach: "Rodman, Gimme the Damn Shirt."

The real upshot of Rodman's indiscretion was that Pippen got nowhere near the rest the team had hoped. Instead, he rushed back into service on March 21, in time to help the Bulls net their 60th win, a satisfying home rout of the Knicks in which Jordan scored 36 with 11 rebounds and five assists. With Pippen back in the lineup, Kukoc moved to power forward and added 12 points and 11 rebounds.

What followed was an upset loss, 109-108, to expansion Toronto and rookie Damon Stoudamire, who scored 30 points. Jordan had 36, but the Bulls' record fell to 60-8.

From there, the Bulls closed out the tumultuous month at 12-2 with two breezy home wins. Kukoc scored 24 to lead them past Atlanta, then Pippen resumed some of his old form with 22 points in a 106-85 defeat of the Clippers.

With the season coming to a close, Kukoc was smiling. Over the seven games he started in Rodman's absence, he had shot 51 percent from the floor and averaged 18.9 points, 6.3 assists, 6.1 rebounds, and 1.4 steals.

The offense was good, but there was a more pressing issue, Jordan said. "Toni's still trying to extend his defensive capabilities and we're going to need his defense in the playoffs," he said. "It'll be just as important as his offense."

"It's an important part of the game," conceded the unabashedly offensive-minded Kukoc. "And I feel I'm playing much better defense than I did my first year. But with me, they bring it up every time I make a mistake. With me, they let me know..."

FAN FAVORITE STEVE KERR.

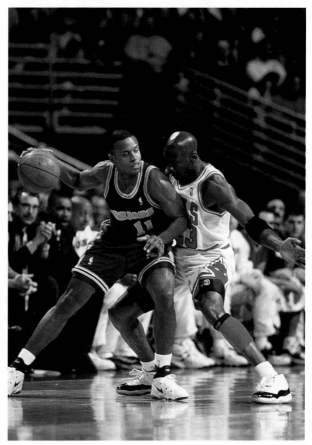

B.J. ARMSTRONG CAME INTO TOWN AT THE END OF MARCH AND HAD A GO AT HIS OLD TEAMMATES, MICHAEL AND SCOTTIE.

8

HE MONTH OF APRIL PRESENTED A series of imposing hurdles for the Bulls, beginning with a first week that included a body-grinding five games in seven nights with two separate road trips to Florida.

JAPAN LOVES YOU, M.J.

MICHAEL'S GLOBAL FOLLOWING SEEMED TO GROW WITH EACH GAME.

At the end of that gauntlet, they faced what was perhaps their most important regular-season contest of the year, an invasion of Orlando, where the Magic were flaunting a consecutive home-win streak to rival the Bulls' own run. The prize from that meeting would be a healthy dose of playoff confidence for the winner.

But before they dealt with the Magic, the Bulls would have to fly to Miami to face the Heat, then jet back to Chicago for a Thursday night rematch with Miami, then get back on their plane to head south again for a Friday night meeting in Charlotte. The capper was a Sunday afternoon game in Orlando on NBC, followed by a Monday night rematch with Charlotte back in Chicago.

Surely a sadist had designed the schedule.

At the very least, the circumstances offered them the opportunity to back off, an excuse to pull up and get ready for the playoffs. But they were riding a wave of pressure and expectations to win 70 games, and for Michael Jordan, backing away from that just wasn't an option.

"History," he said with his jaw set. "That's what this is all about."

Whatever it was, it was good for business. Both WGN and the Sportschannel, the broadcasters for Bulls games, reported their ratings

THE COMBINED COMPETITIVE FIRE OF JORDAN, RODMAN AND PIPPEN DROVE THE BULLS TO THEIR 70TH VICTORY.

at an all-time high. At WGN, the increase was 92 percent. Sportsmart, the sporting goods retailer, reported a similar explosion in sales of the team's merchandise, particularly Jordan and Rodman jerseys, well above the numbers for Jordan's return the previous March, when Bullmania was, well, manic.

"It was crazy before, but it's 10 times crazier now, due primarily to the return of Jordan, the addition of Rodman and the 70-win pace," said Steve Schanwald, the team's vice president for marketing and broadcasting. The Bulls' pull extended around the globe. Busload after busload of tour groups from Japan brought pilgrims willing to pay a minimum of $2,500 apiece to take in a Bulls game, stand by Jordan's statue outside the United Center and drive by Jordan's home north of Chicago.

That the Japanese tourists could get tickets at all was amazing. A VIP seat for a regular-season game was netting nearly $1,000 for scalpers, and a good seat was bringing $400-500. "We're at 109 percent capacity," Schanwald said of seating in the United Center. "And our waiting list for season tickets has grown to 18,500 names from a steady 13,000 for years. We're getting more calls than ever from people desperate to see the Bulls, some of whom are driving to road games to do it."

Area sports bars found themselves entertaining packed houses on game nights. "Something huge is going on, no question about it," Ivan McCullough, manager of Hi-Tops sports bar in Wrigleyville, told the Tribune.

With each home game, the Bulls were adding to their string of consecutive wins, stretching the all-time record to 37, 38, 39. And with every victory, the United Center's reputation as the ultimate home-court advantage took firmer hold. By April, the Bulls' 1995 failings in the building were a distant memory. Now, other NBA teams dreaded being there, dreaded facing the Bulls anywhere for that matter, because it meant an opportunity to get embarrassed with the whole world watching. In fact, NBA players in a *USA Today* poll named the United Center the most difficult place to play in the league.

The circumstances made the away game in Orlando all the more relevant, because the

THE FANS GAVE THE UNITED CENTER A
NEW HOME COURT ADVANTAGE.

TED CENTE

THIS MURAL CAUSED TRAFFIC JAMS AND HAD TO BE REMOVED.

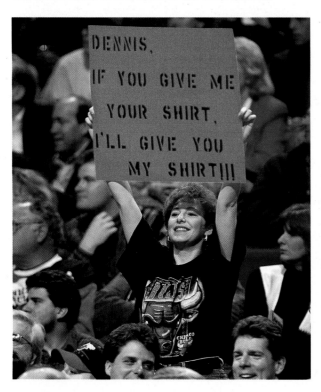

RODMAN SEEMED ALMOST CONTRITE AFTER HIS RETURN FROM SUSPENSION. THE FANS WERE EAGER TO GREET HIM, AND HE RESPONDED WITH HIS USUAL HARD WORK.

THE REVIEWS WERE IN. THE UNITED CENTER HAD SETTLED IN AS THE NEW MADHOUSE ON MADISON, DRAWING SISKEL, ELLE MCPHERSON, OPRAH AND A HOST OF OTHER CELEBRITIES REGULARLY.

THE FIRST WEEK OF APRIL OFFERED A CRAZY SCHEDULE THAT INCLUDED TWO SEPARATE ROAD TRIPS TO FLORIDA.

Magic were fighting neck and neck with Chicago for the all-time consecutive home winning streak, and Michael Jordan was unabashed in his desire to put an end to the string in the O-Rena.

All of this success meant that expectations swelled to tidal proportions as the regular season drew to a close and the Bulls methodically

moved toward their 70th win. The pressure seemed relentless, with the same questions being asked over and over and over each time the Bulls made a public appearance. The situation ate at all of them, but Dennis Rodman admitted that it bothered him perhaps the most.

Dennis returned from his suspension for the road game against

Miami that first week of April and showed up with his hair dyed red, his sixth color change of the season, following red, blond, green, rust, mango, and something of a scramble to open the year.

"I think Dennis looks best as a blond," Jackson mused.

Rodman had spent part of his suspension time with Stone Phillips and a camera crew from NBC's "Dateline" following him around, shooting tape at his hair salon, at Gibson's for dinner and hangin' out at Crobar, one of Chicago's alternative clubs. But he was more concerned with his return.

"It's going to take me a while to get adjusted back to where I used to be," he said in Miami, sounding almost contrite. "I don't expect the team to run up to me and give me respect right now. I have to earn it back and do what I do best. They can win without me. They've done it all year long."

That certainly was true during the regular season. But Jackson knew that his team would come to depend heavily on Rodman's rebounding for the playoffs. So the coach decided to keep Kukoc in the starting lineup, thus ensuring Rodman's hunger each night as he came off the bench.

Pippen and Jordan scored 32 apiece to get the win in Miami, then both teams retreated to Chicago, where the Bulls did it again, this time with a career high 34 from Kukoc and 40 from Jordan.

From there, they jetted down to Charlotte and scored the first 20 points of the game in a laugher over the Hornets. The packed Charlotte Coliseum sat in dead silence watching the destruction of a team fighting to make the playoffs. Late in the game, with the Bulls ahead by a zillion, Rodman was still scrambling around for rebounds. He chased one ball through a scrum, got tripped and still managed to come up with the rebound after an amazing tumble, which he finished by popping to his feet and bowing for the laughing, applauding crowd.

Jackson was clearly right. Dennis was a clown, a rebounding, raving clown.

For the game, Charlotte assistant Johnny Bach had brought his three championship rings from his tenure with the Bulls. Charlotte center Matt Geiger had asked to see the jewelry, and after the game Bach retrieved them from his jacket pocket. They

sparkled in the Coliseum's dimmed lights. Bach eyed them admiringly and said that he thought the Bulls were now playing defense with passion and they seemed well on course to add a fourth ring.

That estimation was comfirmed two days later in Orlando. The Bulls were somewhat disappointed because the Magic had just lost a home game to the visiting Lakers. The Bulls had badly wanted the distinction of ending Orlando's home winning streak. Shaquille O'Neal had taken several games off to attend his grandmother's funeral, but he made a surprise appearance on the Magic bench just after the Bulls game started. His presence, though, wasn't enough to dent the Bulls' progress, even with Luc Longley on the injured list with knee tendinitis.

The game offered a preview of their impending playoff showdown when Jackson decided to assign the 6-8, 225-pound Rodman (who was really closer to 6-7) to cover the 7-1, 330 pound Shaq. The biog guy still scored 21, but the message was clear. Rodman was strong enough to contend with O'Neal.

"I used to live in Oklahoma," Rodman said afterward. "We used to tip cows, 400, 450 pounds. That's not a problem. A lot of guys don't want to play against him. But I don't care. I look forward to the challenge."

Another key factor was Kukoc, who hit five of eight three-point attempts and scored 20 points to help seal the 90-86 win.

Having played their way through the week in dominant fashion, the Bulls soared home and encountered the next unexpected twist, a 98-97 loss to the Hornets. The defeat snapped their home win streak at 44, the all-time record, and ensured that they could do no better than tie the 1986 Celtics for the best home record in a season, at 40-1.

Next came a road win at New Jersey that brought Chicago's record to 67-9 and ensured the home-court advantage for the playoffs. Win

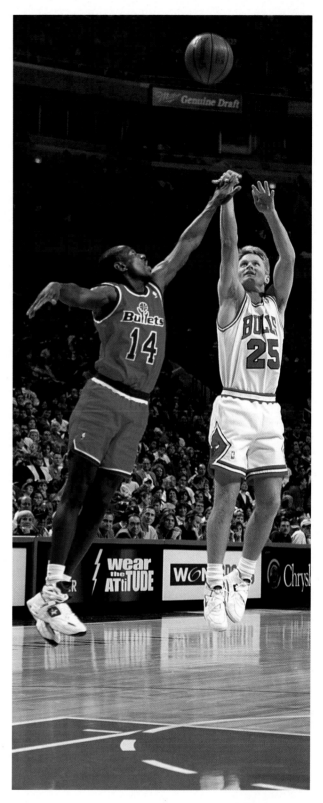

number 68 came by 30 points at the United Center over the lowly Sixers. "The season just keeps dragging on," Rodman said wearily. "I'm ready for the playoffs."

That Sunday, the Bulls went to Cleveland and humiliated the Cavs

THE SHARP-SHOOTING KERR BECAME ONE OF THE BULLS' MANY FAN FAVORITES.

THE BULLS STRUGGLED BUT FINALLY SLAMMED HOME THEIR 70TH WIN IN MILWAUKEE.

JACK HALEY GOT TO PLAY IN THE VERY LAST REGULAR-SEASON GAME, IN WASHINGTON.

of the historic game right from the very start. But that just didn't happen. In fact, the Bucks still held a lead late in the third quarter, and the fourth opened with a heated battle for the momentum.

Was this the way to make history? Actually, the Bulls would take it any way they could get it, especially on a night when Jordan and Pippen made only 16 of 46 shots. "We came out totally lackluster," Jordan admitted later.

The key, as had become increasingly clear over the course of the season, was the Bulls' defense. Their pressure worked on the Bucks, then Steve Kerr came in to fire the fatal shots, a three-pointer, another deep jumper, and clutch free throws in the last minute.

It was the kind of performance Kerr had turned in all season long. The NBA's all-time leader in three-point field goal percentage, he was one of only two players in the league to hit better than 50 percent of his three-point attempts, and he shot .927 from the free-throw line. Fouled with 13 seconds to go in the game, Kerr had laughed, confident that the 70th win was in hand because he knew the free throws were good.

It wasn't arrogance, but experience, that brought the response. Each and every day of practice he shot 100 free throws, something no other Bull, not even Jordan, had the drive to do.

"It takes a long time," Kerr said of the effort needed to develop as a shooter. "I've been shooting literally since I was five or six years old. I got really serious about it in high school. I started working out and doing drills. The reason I can do it now is because I've been working on it for 25 years."

After stops in Cleveland and Orlando, Kerr seemed to have found an NBA home in Chicago. Jordan appeared to be comfortable playing with him and encouraged him to be aggressive with his shot. The fact that it was Kerr down the stretch who delivered enough offense for the

on national television to tie the Lakers' 69-win record. Jordan led the effort with 32 points and 12 rebounds.

Pippen, who had been touted as the league MVP much of the season, was asked who should get the award. "Michael," he said without hesitation. "There's no one standing near him that can compare to the type of season he's played, the numbers he's put up. It's not even a close race."

About the only unanswered ques-tion as the Bulls headed to Milwaukee seeking win number 70 on Tuesday, April 16 was the color of Rodman's hair. A few days into his return, he had taken Jackson's sug-gestion and reverted to blond, but with a swirling red streak. Then, headed into the team's historic week, he had opted for a Flamingo pink, as if the fans needed a reminder that the Bulls were sitting pretty.

Scottie Pippen had wanted to make sure they took Milwaukee out struggling Bulls to get their 70th win only reinforced his position.

Another interesting item to emerge from the celebration that night was the fact that the first person Pippen hugged after it was over was Rodman.

"I have no problem with Dennis," Pippen explained later. "Our on-court relationship is fine. He has been dedicated to this team, and we've shared the same goals. You don't have to be close off the court to bond on it."

If the Bulls were hoping their 70th win would put to rest the questions about their place in history, they were sadly mistaken. If anything, the debate intensified. The Lakers' Jerry West said that he'd had so many calls about comparing the '72 Lakers with the '96 Bulls that he found it almost unbearable to talk about it.

Ron Harper helped put off some of the speculation by coining the phrase, "Don't Mean A Thing Without The Ring." In other words, the Bulls would have to close the season with a championship.

Otherwise, their regular-season victory total would be hollow.

Before the playoffs, however, the Bulls faced the short-term goal of closing out the season with a 40-1 home record. They got their 71st win over the Pistons at the United Center but lost Harper with a severely sprained left ankle.

Their last regular-season home game on Saturday the 20th against the Indiana Pacers came down to a final scramble. Jackson rested his starters most of the game, but Jordan played big minutes in the fourth quarter. "Come on, Mike," Jackson yelled from the bench. "Finish this, OK?"

Jordan tried, but a last-second whistle from official Hue Hollins sent Indiana to the free-throw line for a 100-99 victory, a scene reminiscent of Hollins' late call against Pippen in the 1994 playoffs against New York. Jordan was furious afterward. "I wanted that really badly," he

said. "That (tying the Celtics' record) would have been another notch in our belt. But I just wanted to continue to win at home. I don't want to give any teams any added motivation."

Still fuming, the Bulls traveled to Washington for the season's last game and tallied their 72nd win with a 103-93 victory at USAir Arena, a game that even featured a few minutes playing time for Jack Haley. As a final touch, Jackson had invited Senator Bill Bradley, his old Knicks teammate, to speak to the team immediately after the game.

Encountered outside the locker room just before his talk, Bradley was asked how this Bulls team would stack up against the Lakers, Knicks and other '70s teams. The Bulls would fare well, especially when you look at the matchups, Bradley said.

"Our Knicks team would match up pretty well until you got to small forward. Then I'd be matched with

Scottie Pippen, and I'd be yelling, 'Help!' "

Actually that would be no worse than what the Bulls' contemporary opponents faced. Jordan, in particular, had been relentless, playing in every game, averaging 30.4 points on 49.5 percent shooting from the floor.

"It's a nice number, 72-10," Jackson said in his post-game remarks. "It rings well."

The coach was fully aware of the pun he had launched. Indeed, they all hoped it would ring well. Standing in their immediate path was Pat Riley and the Miami Heat, their first round playoff opponent.

"I think Miami's thrown the gauntlet a little bit, and let it be known that they're ready for us," Jackson said.

Jordan, though, would have none of that talk. "The only way we can lose," he said, "is if we beat ourselves."

JACKSON HAD HIS OLD KNICKS TEAMMATE, BILL BRADLEY, SPEAK TO THE TEAM AFTER VICTORY NUMBER 72.

THE COACHES WERE CONFIDENT THAT THE BULLS DEFENSE COULD TAKE AWAY MOURNING'S PET MOVE.

THE HEAT HAD NO ANSWER FOR JORDAN AND COMPANY.

T WASN'T THAT THE BULLS HAD AN inflated confidence. But they knew that they could handle Miami Heat center Alonzo Mourning in the postseason. They knew what to expect from Mourning because they had also opened the 1995 playoffs against him, when he was a Charlotte Hornet.

To plan their strategy against Mourning a year earlier, the Bulls coaching staff had gathered in their war room at the team's practice facility, the Berto Center, in north suburban Chicago. Evidence of Phil Jackson's Native American interests abound in this inner sanctum, including an owl feather and a bearclaw necklace. There were pictures of the sacred white buffalo calf and of Crazy Horse. On one wall hung an arrow with a tobacco pouch. These were here for more than effect, but the real focus of the room was the video monitor.

Assistant coach Jim Cleamons had broken down videotape of the Hornets into a scouting report. One of their first observations was that the 6-10 Mourning was somewhat clumsy and traveled nearly every time he got the ball in the post.

"He walks on everything," complained Tex Winter. "He's got big ole feet. He can't help but walk."

Cleamons had included a selection of tape showing Mourning caught in a triple team yet forcing up a terrible shot instead of passing. "He wants to be the hero," Cleamons noted.

Mourning's shortcomings aside, the Bulls knew they would have to double-team him and take away his pet move in the low post.

"Mourning will still have all of our post guys in foul trouble," cautioned Winter, an inveterate worrier.

"That's all right. We have 18 fouls to give," Jackson said.

"But Mourning's a good foul shooter," Winter said, not satisfied. "We've got to figure how to keep the ball out of that guy's hands."

Such debate was a welcomed and critical element of Chicago's coaching approach, and it resulted in the Bulls handling Mourning with relative ease in 1995. For 1996, the Chicago coaches knew they would face the same Alonzo Mourning. But this year he was allied with perhaps the Bulls' biggest rival, coach Pat Riley, who, while coach of the New York Knicks, had engaged Jackson in a personal competition that only heightened the team matchups. Earlier in the year, after the Bulls had been upset by Riley's new Heat team, Jackson had come into the locker room and told his players, "Never lose to that guy."

Now, some people around the NBA were speculating that Riley might inflame his Miami club for the playoffs with the same bruising style his Knicks teams had featured.

"They're not New York," Jackson said of the Heat roster. "They don't have Mason, Oakley, and Ewing. They can't play that game."

That didn't mean the Heat wouldn't try. In fact, as the regular season came to a close, Dennis Rodman had warned that Riley might use certain players as intimidators to instigate trouble to "get inside my head and get me ejected. But that's not going to happen."

Riley and the Heat players shared a snicker over this accusation, beause Rodman enjoyed quite a reputation as an instigator himself. Veteran Bulls fans, in fact, could well recall Rodman's antics from his Piston days, which made them all the happier to see him in a Bulls uniform.

Rodman, however, was far from being alone in this posturing. The days leading up to the first round brought a war of quotes and sound bites between Mourning and Riley on one side, Jackson and Pippen on the other. Scottie and Mourning, in particular, had directed

DESPITE A BAD BACK AND BAD ANKLES, PIPPEN STILL WENT TO THE RACK IN TRAFFIC.

macho insinuations at one another until, finally, Pippen relented and said that "all the questions will be answered on the basketball court."

"They can talk," Mourning retorted. "That's arrogance. But they're not invincible."

Jordan seemed to agree. In the time prior to the first round, he was as nervous as a rookie. "We have a lot to prove as a team," he said.

It's not pretty, the dissection of proud people. And they don't come any prouder than Riley and Mourning. But that's essentially what happened in the best-of-five first round. The Bulls made it seem like a clinic, beginning with the very first

moments of Game 1, when the United Center crowd greeted Mourning with thunderous booing during introductions.

Once the Heat had endured the disrespect of the Chicago fans, the house lights went dark, and those familiar riffs from Allan Parsons Project's "Eye In The Sky" started tingling through the building, followed by another deafening outburst from the fans, a gush of energy aimed at getting the Bulls off to a big start on their playoff run.

There on the floor during introductions, Benny the Bull was down on all fours, bowing and scraping and worshipping, as announcer Ray Clay introduced the starters. The only mild surprise was that Jackson decided to keep Kukoc in the starting lineup and bring Rodman off the bench.

Riley had his Heat pumped to a high intensity, but Mourning's fury to open the game earned him only two quick fouls, and from there the first period went awry for the Heat, who drew three technical fouls and gave up 29 points.

With Mourning on the bench in foul trouble much of the first half, the Heat relied on point guard Tim Hardaway to provide the offense. He responded with 20 points in the second period, scoring inside and out, and drove Miami into the lead. But a late basket by Bulls reserve Randy Brown tied it at 54 at the half, and that was as close as Miami would get to being competitive.

Ron Harper had struggled with a badly sprained ankle at the end of the regular season, but he showed no lack of mobility in the second half in shutting down Hardaway, a Chicago native. That left the Heat with little offense, because Mourning continued his bone-headed challenging of the officials and was ejected by official Steve Javie in the fourth period.

Before leaving the floor, Mourning stopped to jaw with Pippen face to face. Moments later, Javie ejected Riley, and toward the end of the period Miami's Chris Gatling also got tossed.

The Bulls closed it out convincingly, 102-85, with Jordan scoring 35 on 13-for-22 shooting. At power forward, Kukoc had 21 points, while Pippen scored 13 with eight rebounds.

Pippen conceded afterward that the Bulls had been a bit anxious, but it was obvious there was little reason

to worry.

The Bulls opened Game 2 on April 27 with Jay Leno sitting courtside. It was clacker night – perhaps the most obnoxious of NBA promotions – at the United Center, and when Mourning drew an early shooting foul, the arena clacked in anticipation, then broke into a rattling delirium when he missed. When Mourning missed his second, the clackers climbed yet another notch on the annoyance scale.

Moments later, when Mourning drew another shooting foul, the clackers were waiting, and when he missed yet again, the whole building was transformed into a giant

MICHAEL SCORCHED PAT RILEY'S HEAT.

Scott Cunningham/NBA photo

PAT RILEY AND ALONZO MOURNING WERE BOTH EJECTED IN THE FIRST PLAYOFF GAME.

squawking nest, rattling with delight.

Always a man with a sense of timing, Jackson chose the pause between free throws as the moment to introduce Rodman into the game. Just the sight of him brought the usual large round of cheers, which perhaps prompted Mourning into missing his fourth straight free throw.

Whatever the effect of all of this,

the net result was a terrible start for the Heat, one from which they never recovered. Miami trailed 60-38 at the half. As both teams left the floor, Ron Harper jokingly bumped Heat reserve Jeff Malone, who was in street clothes.

Angry, Mourning hit Harper with a towel. "I wasn't in a joking mood," the Miami center said later.

The reason for that was Jordan. His patent-leather shoes with their rubbery sheen made it look like Mike was playing in galoshes. His game, however, showed no encumbrances. By midway through the second quarter, he had bedazzled the Heat with 26 points.

But Michael's big show came to a halt late in the period when he suf-

RODMAN DID A WACKY SHOW WITH JAY LENO AS THE PLAYOFFS OPENED.

RODMAN HAD EVERYONE TALKING WHEN HE SHOWED UP FOR A BOOK SIGNING IN DRAG.

fered a strained back as he was fouled on a reverse layup from the left baseline. He landed awkwardly, and it was immediately apparent that he was in pain, first because Jordan, who has a high tolerance for pain, rarely ever acknowledges any. This time, though, he was showing it, and trainer Chip Schaefer came onto the floor to check him out before the free throw attempts.

Jordan shook him off, but moments later headed to the locker room for evaluation and treatment. That alone signalled to the crowd that maybe there was trouble. Jordan later returned, but the back pain would nag him through the next two rounds.

The only other fireworks in the second half came with Rodman's ejection for a hard foul on Mourning, his second technical. Other than that, it was all slow-mo, a 106-75 win for a 2-0 Bulls lead.

The Heat didn't score 20 points in any of the four quarters and shot only 35 percent from the floor. Miami starting forwards Walt Williams and Kurt Thomas were held scoreless, and Mourning finished with 14.

"It's almost as if our guys came in here and apologized for playing hard the other night," Riley said afterward. "That's the sense I got. I just thought we were very soft."

Jordan had scored just three points in the third period and sat out the fourth to finish with 29. The Bulls' other big performance came from Pippen, who had 24 points, eight rebounds and eight assists.

"We're going to try and get this over as soon as possible," Jackson said afterward.

True to that intent, the Bulls scored 37 points in the first quarter of Game 3 at Miami Arena. Mourning finally broke free of the defensive net Chicago had thrown over him and scored 30 points, but the game was never in question.

Pippen provided the power with a monster triple-double, the 17th of his career, including four in the play-

BULLS FANS KNEW WHERE THEIR TEAM WAS HEADED.

KUKOC WAS NAMED THE SIXTH MAN OF THE YEAR, A ROLE HE HADN'T EXACTLY WANTED.

offs. He finished with 22 points, 18 rebounds and 10 assists as the Bulls completed the sweep, 112-91.

Jordan led the effort with 26, but his ginger steps up and down the court showed just how much his back bothered him. He had been unable to sleep the night before. "But once I got out there, I played," he said. "Every now and then when I twisted it, I could feel the pull. It's going to take a couple more days to get some more treatment and hopefully it will dissolve."

Next up were the New York Knicks, who had easily dismissed the Cleveland Cavaliers. If anybody in the NBA knew how to play the Bulls, knew how to interrupt the triple-post offense, it was New York, the team that had presented itself as an annual playoff hurdle. As Pippen told reporters, the going would soon get very tough for the Bulls.

They were about to face the bump and run.

JORDAN GETTING PREPPED FOR BATTLE.

HOW UGLY WAS THE BULLS' SECOND-round playoff series with the New York Knicks?

To watch this segment of Air Chicago's flight to the 1996 NBA Finals, you needed one of those little white air sickness bags. Maybe two of them. This, of course, was nothing unusual. The Bulls and Knicks had met eight times in the playoffs during the Jordan era, and every one of them invoked visions of Wrestlemania. For much of that time, Pat Riley had been the Knicks' coach and had worked them into a package of intimidation. But with Riley's departure to Miami the previous summer, New York had hired veteran NBA coach Don Nelson, only to fire him a few months later and replace him with assistant Jeff Van Gundy, a Riley disciple in his first pro head coaching job.

Chicago Tribune columnist Bernie Lincicome described Van Gundy as a "sad-eyed mortician," but appearances were deceiving. Van Gundy had the Knicks playing well, with that old Riley intensity, which meant they were meeting finesse with muscle.

"They're a tough team," observed Bulls reserve John Salley. "Derek Harper is one of the best defensive guards in the world. Patrick Ewing is definitely a force in the middle. You got Oakley and Mason, who are strong as two oxen. You got Starks, who's playing well since the first round, and you got those guys off the bench who are playing their roles and liking it."

Most important, this collection of Knicks had played together for a few years now, and they knew how to pressure the Bulls. On the other hand, the Bulls understood what it took to beat New York.

Mostly, the series would prove that, in pro basketball, familiarity breeds frustration. Neither team had much luck executing its offense. Knowing that the stakes had risen considerably, Jackson decided to move Rodman back into the starting lineup, with Kukoc, caught in a spiraling slump, coming off the bench.

Rodman pre-empted this news with a blast of flamboyance, arriving in drag and wearing a feather boa at a promotional appearance for his new book, "Bad As I Wanna Be," at a Miracle Mile bookstore on the eve of the Knicks series.

The crowd and traffic jams and ensuing video clips of the event turned the city, not to mention Bulls' management, on its ear. A great admirer of radio shock jock Howard Stern, Rodman had planned to promote his own book in drag, just as Stern had with his recent bestselling titles. While some were wondering if Dennis hadn't crossed the line, his teammates took the event with a sense of humor.

"He went in and talked about not being homophobic, about cross dressing," said Salley, who had known Rodman since their rookie season together as Pistons. "When his unisex, bisexual line of clothing comes out, everybody's gonna buy it. 'Who's this for?' they'll ask. 'It depends on the night, honey.' "

Prompted by reporters for a more definitive endorsement of Rodman, Salley reassured them, "He's strictly all male." Then he added, "He looked great, kinda pretty."

Salley explained that despite appearances, the only real transformation that Rodman had made was "that he understands the game now. I mean the marketing game, the business game. He's a shy guy, so what he's doing, one of the ways he's coming out of being an introvert, is to be an extrovert with his image."

Hmmm.

"Dennis is winking at the world," explained Bulls vice president Steve Schanwald.

As far as basketball was concerned, the big issue in Chicago leading into Game 1 on Sunday, May 5, was the status of Jordan's back. As he emerged from the Bulls' huddle to start the game, Jordan did a little hop while patty-caking his hands. This little jump served as a signal to United Center crowd that once again

AND OPRAH WAS READY TO GET THE SHIRT.

THE KNICKS WERE READY TO GET PHYSICAL.

PIPPEN AND RODMAN CONTENDED WITH THE KNICKS DOWN LOW.

he was ready to play, that a little something like a bad back wasn't going to stop him.

The Knicks controlled the opening tip and quickly scored on a Charles Oakley layup, but Jordan answered with a trey. Moments later, Rodman crisply snagged a defensive rebound and fired an outlet to Jordan, who ambled a few yards and

stuck a pullup jumper, five quick points on his way to a 15-point first quarter and a 25-point half.

For the Knicks, the message was clear. MJ was going to do it to them yet again, as he had time after time over the years. So many times, in fact, that "it" had left the nation's sportswriters and broadcasters struggling for metaphors to capture just how it felt.

George Vecsey of the New York Times likened it to surgery without anesthesia. For the Knicks, it felt worse than that. Their response in the first half of Game 1 was the usual stuff, a good stiff physical style.

Late in the first period, Jordan was giving them the deluxe workout when he suddenly broke free for a drive from the left. Intent on stop-

JORDAN DID YEOMAN WORK ON DEFENSE, INCLUDING THIS TUSSLE WITH THE KNICKS' DEREK HARPER.

JERRY KRAUSE, THE EXECUTIVE OF THE YEAR, CONGRATULATES JACKSON, THE COACH OF THE YEAR.

ping him, Ewing lunged across the lane and nailed Jordan in the solar plexus just as he was elevating to slam. Jordan flinched in pain and the ball struck the underside of the rim, but there was no call, which left Michael under the basket punching the air in fury as play headed the other way.

The Bulls opened a 15-point lead early on, but Ewing himself turned in a splendid half offensively, his 14 points combining with Derek Harper's 10 to pull New York within 54-47 by intermission.

From there, New York managed to pull even in the second half, mainly by taking the Bulls out of their offense.

"What they're doing is spreading their defense," Tex Winter said of the Knicks. "They also space our offense. They spread our offense. But we don't mind that. That's part of our concept. It opens up the basket area for cuts and for rebounds."

Yet the Bulls weren't able to take advantage of the circumstances because they were shooting poorly, missing open shots, a trend that

would continue throughout the series.

The opening session pretty much summed up the much-predicted nature of the series. The Knicks, veteran team that they were, would respond with a tough-minded performance, but in the end it did little more than keep them from being embarrassed.

As always, Michael dominated the proceedings with his pirouettes and jab steps and fallaway jumpers and dunks. He presented a mountain of talent, and the Knicks had no hopes of scaling it. Jordan finished Game 1 with 44 points, the 31st time he had scored more than 40 in a playoff game.

The other factor was the vaunted Chicago defense, which forced 17 turnovers and did not allow the Knicks a field goal over the final five minutes of the game. That was enough for a 91-84 win and a 1-0 lead in the series.

"We could not have played much worse," Steve Kerr said. "It was just a case of riding on Michael's shoulders. We didn't get much out of anybody."

The second game proved to be remarkably similar, except that

Chicago got more balanced scoring with Jordan waiting until seven minutes had gone by before taking a shot.

Ewing again led New York with 23 points, but scored just one in the fourth quarter when the Bulls were applying the pressure. "I think our defensive intensity, our focus down the stretch at the end of the game, is really putting pressure on them to find some offense," Pippen said. "We've been able to shut them down when they need offense."

This time, the Bulls' defensive heat produced 20 Knicks turnovers and nearly an eight-minute cold spell in the fourth quarter as Chicago took over for a 91-80 win and a 2-0 series lead.

Ron Harper once more was vital to the pressure on defense, and Harper also added 15 points to go with Jordan's 28 and Pippen's 19.

"He's been terrific, especially his floor game," Tex Winter said of Harper. "His shooting's been a little erratic, but good enough to maintain a threat. One thing about Harper, he may go out there and miss eight or

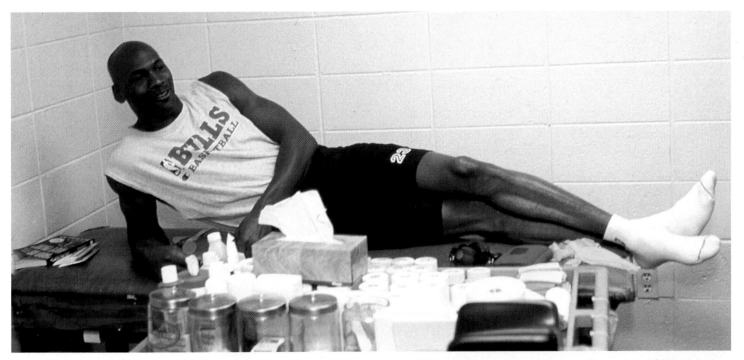

JORDAN AND PIPPEN NURSED BAD BACKS.

10 good open shots. It doesn't seem to bother him much. He just keeps plugging and keeps playing that defense."

Another key to the victory was Rodman's 19 rebounds. "It's amazing to watch him control the game just by rebounding," Steve Kerr said afterward.

Without question, Rodman's presence was a welcome relief. He had struggled to get in sync in the Miami series. The Bulls badly needed him to counter the Knicks' musclebound frontcourt, which easily brushed aside Kukoc, who was ailing from back problems and would miss the third and fourth games of the series.

Fortunately, New York still hadn't played well offensively. But that changed for Game 3, a Saturday afternoon meeting in New York. John Starks scored 30, and the Knicks bumped their way to an 80-69 lead with six minutes left.

During the New York run, referee Hue Hollins had inadvertently staggered Van Gundy with a blow to the head while signalling a three-second call against Chicago.

The Knicks coach struggled to his feet and waited for the next shot, delivered by Jordan, who came alive over the final six minutes, driving the Bulls into a tie with eight points in the final 71 seconds of regulation – including two deep three-pointers and a magnificent jumper with Starks and Mason sandwiching him in midair.

Jordan scored 46 points in 51 minutes of playing time, but there just wasn't enough help. The Knicks survived in overtime, 102-99, and pulled the series to 2-1.

Suddenly, the Bulls were vulnerable. Jordan was hurt and exhausted, and they faced Game 4 less than 24 hours away.

LONGLEY HELPED
WITH DEFENSE, AND
BUDDHA PROVIDED
SPOT OFFENSE.

The Bulls coaches hurriedly studied the game tape, and Tex Winter came away unconvinced it was the Knicks' defense causing all the trouble.

"We got an awful lot of shots we just didn't hit," Winter said. The Knicks were cleverly "snakebiting," or hitting Jordan and his teammates with a flick on the elbow as they released their shots. "Pretty soon, whether they foul you or not, you're worrying about it, or anticipating they might, and that throws your shooting off," Winter said.

Things looked poor for Game 4 with Kukoc out and Jordan exhausted. Then Pippen wrenched his back in the first half, and the pressure

mounted on Chicago. Jordan played 40 minutes but suffered through a 7-for-23 afternoon.

The answers came from Harper, who scored 18 points, from Rodman, who had 19 more rebounds and two crucial fourth-quarter assists, and from Bill Wennington, who finished those assists with big baskets in the last two minutes to push the Bulls out of danger.

"Dennis got me the ball, I was open, and I hit the shot," Wennington said matter of factly, although he was privately elated over his contribution, which lifted the Bulls to a 94-91 win and a 3-1 series lead.

The Bulls had surrendered the

rebounding edge in Game 3, but Rodman led the effort to reclaim it in Game 4, and Jackson figured that made the difference.

"We didn't shoot well, but we were able to divide the rebounds," the Bulls' Zen specialist said afterward.

What made the loss hard for the Knicks was a traveling call in the final seconds, just before Starks nailed a three-pointer that would have tied it. "I thought it was a good shot – no steps," he said.

Headed back to Chicago for Game 5, the Knicks knew their best chances had passed. Yet closing the series out would require one final round of sacrifices from the Bulls. Pippen would have to dive on the

floor for loose balls despite his troublesome back. Ron Harper would have to shake off the stomach flu.

Mostly, though, Jordan would have to come back with 35 points, and it was the Bulls' good fortune that all of those things happened as they closed out business, 94-81.

The difference was seven points apiece from Pippen and Jordan in the third period as Chicago seized control, which meant that when Rodman got tossed in the fourth quarter for a second technical, the outcome was already decided. Dennis paraded past the New York bench and tossed his jersey into the stands with the finality of, say, Red Auerbach lighting a cigar.

"We knew that it was going to be this kind of a series and that we were going to have to get into a slugfest," Jackson said. "We knew it was going to be a battle."

It wasn't pretty, but the Bulls had survived, and now they could get down to the business they'd been planning for all year. Now they could have another go at Orlando.

SCOTTIE PUT THE FINISHING FLOURISH ON A BULLS FAST BREAK AGAINST THE KNICKS.

O SAY THE LEAST, ANXIETY WAS HIGH in Chicago as the Bulls prepared to meet the Orlando Magic for the 1996 Eastern Conference Championship. Like the Bulls, Shaquille O'Neal and the Magic had moved through the first two rounds of competition with a glitzy 7-1 record. But unlike Chicago, Orlando had barely struggled against Detroit and Atlanta. The Bulls, meanwhile, had emerged from their series with New York battered and bruised and looking like a team that might not have the gas to get over the hump.

As usual, Chicago's designated worrier was Tex Winter.

"We've got to have a good shooting percentage out of Scottie and Michael," the 73-year-old assistant said as the series was set to open. "Otherwise, we're not going to have enough scoring to contest this ballclub."

Added to those concerns were the team's injuries. Jordan, Pippen and Kukoc, the Bulls' three leading scorers, all had aching backs. Pippen's ankles were in terrible shape, and Ron Harper was beginning to experience problems with his reconstructed knees.

And now, the Bulls' 72-win season added immense pressure on Jordan and his teammates. "That's on everybody's mind," Winter said. "The press talks about it. The players feel it. Now that we've got that history-breaking 72 wins, the pressure is on us. We've got to go out and win the championship. The worst thing you can do in this business is disappoint peo-

MICHAELANGELO.

THIS TIME AROUND, HORACE GRANT COULD ONLY WATCH AS PIPPEN AND THE BULLS SOARED TO A SWEEP.

ple. These guys don't want to disappoint people, especially themselves."

Avoiding that would require that the Bulls find better shot selection than they had shown against the Knicks. "And Dennis has got to become a little more offensive-minded for us," Winter said. "He needs to go ahead and carry the threat and make them play him, not let them ignore him totally, not let them run off and leave him and double Michael without making them play."

On the upside, Winter figured the Bulls would be able to move the ball with more freedom against Orlando. The Magic had the athletes to play good pressure defense, but they didn't play it with New York's 48-minute intensity.

"They pace themselves," Winter said. "They kind of turn it on and off."

Jackson, on the other hand, wanted to make sure the Bulls kept their intensity up all the time. In preparing for Orlando, he had spliced select scenes from the film "Pulp Fiction," a black comedy about hired killers, in between sections of Magic videotape. The message was clear: He wanted Chicago to finish off the Magic like cold-blooded assasins.

After all, this was the same Magic team that had humiliated and embarrassed them in last year's playoffs. Jackson wanted to ignite the legendary killer instinct in Michael Jordan. His attitude infused the entire Bulls roster, many of whom had never played on teams that had reached the rare air of the conference finals.

Jackson was also concerned that Jordan might try to do too much, leaving his teammates out. Nevertheless, Jackson knew he had to have his players thinking like killers and he had to make it fun. The scenes from "Pulp Fiction" did just the trick.

"They're a very loose group, a very relaxed group," Winter admitted. "They have a lot of confidence in themselves."

The Bulls certainly came out like killers in Game 1 on May 19 at the United Center. The morning's Sun Times ran a front-page section comparing Rodman with Orlando's Horace Grant. One of the stories, written by an Orlando writer, suggested that Grant was the better power forward because he scored more.

Did the Worm need any greater motivation?

Apparently not.

During his career as a little-used journeyman with Atlanta and Denver, Scott Hastings had come up with the concept of the "trillion," his designation for minutes of action during which a player contributed absolutely nothing statistically to his team's effort.

For example, a player might go five minutes without a point, shot, rebound, even a foul. Such performances would read like 5-000-000-000-000 in the box score. Hastings had registered a few trillion over his career, and he had even recalled seeing a player once manage 14 trillion in one game. Hastings wondered how that could happen.

That certainly would be a question worth asking the Magic players after the Rodman-Grant collision in Game 1.

In the days leading up to the series, Grant's warrior attitude had been cited as the source of Orlando's leadership, but Rodman erased any such thoughts over the first three periods of Game 1.

During that time, Grant registered an amazing 28 trillion that included one missed shot, one rebound and one foul.

It was almost an act of mercy when Grant hyperextended his elbow during a collision with O'Neal. Never had an NBA star been so completely taken out of a game as Grant had been by Rodman.

Dennis, meanwhile, had 21 rebounds and complied with his coaches' request for more scoring with 13 points. His effort led a charge that saw the Bulls outrebound Orlando, 62-28. The final score, 121-83, reflected just how overwhelmed the Magic were. While Longley contended with O'Neal in the post, Harper, Jordan and Pippen shut down the rest of the Magic line-

GRANT WAS FORCED TO SIT OUT WITH AN INJURED ELBOW.

up. Dennis Scott failed to score, and Nick Anderson missed all seven shots from the field and managed just two free throws.

The Bulls, on the other hand, used balanced scoring to blow open the game in the third period with a 16-2 run. Jordan finished with 21, Pippen 18 and Longley 14, while Kerr and Kukoc led a dominant

Chicago bench with 14 and 12 points respectively.

"They dominated the boards on us," Orlando coach Brian Hill said glumly. "Rebounding is nothing but effort and concentration. It's obviously something we have to correct."

Asked how he could counter Rodman, Hill said, "The only way you counter Dennis Rodman is to

get somebody out there who works as hard as he does. Quite honestly, there aren't a lot of guys in the game of basketball who do that."

The terrible news for Orlando was that Grant would be lost for the remainder of the series. While the Magic coaches fretted over their adjustments for Game 2, the Bulls steadied themselves to receive yet

WENNINGTON WITH AUTHORITY.

RODMAN CONTROLLED THE BOARDS AND THE OUTCOME.

another in a brace of awards coming their way in this historic season. Pippen, Jordan and Rodman had all been named to the NBA's all-defense first team. Jackson was named the league's coach of the year for the first time. Kukoc claimed the Sixth Man Award, and Krause was named executive of the year by The Sporting News.

The capstone to these achieve-

ments was Jordan winning the league MVP award, his fourth.

"(Coaching) Michael is like coaching Michaelangelo, genius at work," Jackson said at the award presentation at a hotel north of Chicago. "No one deserves this more."

"Two or three years ago, I would never have dreamed of being in this position again," Jordan said. "Quite honestly, Phil and I sat down and we

tried to come up with a reason how I could be back in this position again, and if he remembers correctly, he couldn't convince me at the time, and I just had to walk away from the game.

"For my reasons personally as well as publicly, I made the right decision. And when I made the right decision to come back, I came back with the notion of being part of the Chicago

JACKSON AND JORDAN TALKED OVER THINGS IN ORLANDO.

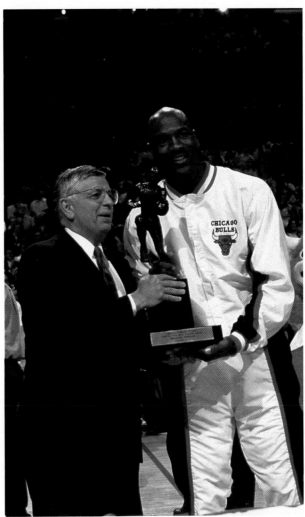

STERN PRESENTED JORDAN THE LEAGUE MVP.

Bulls organization, with Phil and Scottie, and to get ourselves and the city back on top."

But getting back there would require more climbing from the Bulls. They knew that without Grant the Magic would still lash back with a major effort in Game 2. The Bulls would have to answer, and to do that, they hoped for more from Kukoc, who was mired in a one-for-27 slump from three-point range.

"Despite the slump, it's something he feels like he can do," Winter said of Kukoc's long-range shooting. "Subsequently, it's some-thing he will do."

Kerr, who had smoked the Magic by making four of five three-point attempts in Game 1, offered Kukoc a ready solution to the problem. "Throw me the ball," he joked.

The laughing, however, quickly stopped in Game 2. Shaq scored 36 and mounted a serious attack in the first half, and by midway through the third quarter, Orlando had pushed its lead to 18. Behind 65-48, the Bulls turned to their defense and held Orlando scoreless for nearly four minutes. Their 10-0 run pulled them to 65-58 with just under three minutes left in the period. Then they turned the pressure on again and stopped the Magic time and again over the last two minutes of the period, which Jordan closed out with a 12-foot jumper to pull Chicago within 69-67.

PIPPEN SHOWS SOME AIR IN
A WIN OVER THE MAGIC.

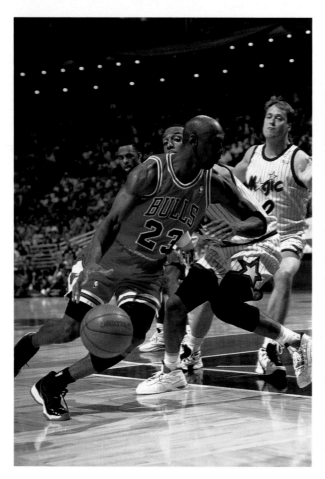

MICHAEL WAS AFIRE IN GAME 4, SCORING 45 AND SENDING THE MAGIC TO AN EARLY END.

The panic was obvious in the Magic's eyes.

"We lost our poise," Orlando point guard Anfernee Hardaway admitted. He had scored 38 in Game 1, but the Bulls' defense held him to 18 in Game 2.

The Bulls gained the lead two minutes into the fourth quarter, but Orlando fought back and regained it, 79-76. A year earlier, the Bulls had lost to Orlando by failing to execute in the final minutes of close games. Now the tables reversed themselves. With Kerr dropping in a key jumper, Randy Brown putting in clutch free throws and the pressure defense working like a blueprint, the Bulls completed their comeback and held off the Magic, 93-88.

Surrendering the big lead was obviously a downer for Orlando. "I think that's something they're going to be thinking about," Jordan said slyly. He had scored 25 of his 35 points during the second-half stampede.

Rodman had scored 15 points

with 12 rebounds, while Pippen just missed a triple double with 17 points, 10 rebounds and nine assists.

Winter was perhaps proudest of Kerr. "People talk about, 'Well, he can't get shots; he only gets two or three shots a ballgame.' But if he does get three or four shots, he might hit two of them, and they might be three-pointers. But the big thing is, they have to guard him. The reason he can't get shots is because they've got somebody occupied on defense, and that creates the opening for Michael and Pippen and everybody else. That's what people don't realize sometimes about the game. You've got to keep people occupied."

The Magic were plenty occupied. Down 2-0, they returned home for

Game 3 with a growing injury list. Jon Koncak, Grant's backup, had injured his knee in Game 2, and Brian Shaw awakened the morning of the third game with a strained neck.

Bulls officials, meanwhile, spent the evening before Game 3 fishing in the pond at the villas where the team was sequestered. They weren't about to celebrate early, but it did seem they were on their way to landing another big one.

Two hours before game time, Koncak took the floor to give his knee a test run. He took several tippy-toe jump shots, then ran up and down the floor a few times with the team's strength coach. The cortisone shot he had taken seemed to be working, which meant he would play.

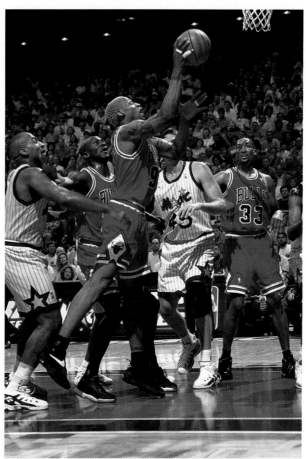

RODMAN AND HARPER PROVIDED UNEXPECTED OFFENSIVE CONTRIBUTIONS.

In the Bulls locker room, Rodman sat alone, a black head rag covering his hairdo, arms folded, legs crossed, ears stuffed between headphones, listening to Pearl Jam. Pippen was perched across the room in a quietly nasty mood, angry with the media, an indication that he was ready to erase any doubts about the outcome.

About the only person talking was Ron Harper, who played a critical role in the pressure defense, because he usually took the other team's hottest scorer. "MJ and Scottie, they are very good defensive basketball players, and they like to be free to chase the basketball," Harper said. "So if their player gets a hot hand because they chase the basketball, then I'll probably change to that guy. And they'll switch to the guy who's not playing good, so they can be free. I don't mind that. Those two guys will hound the ball and do a fine job at it. Those guys will chase the ball 'til the sun goes down."

This pressure was merciless against Orlando's shorthanded guards in Game 3. The Magic were held to 67 points, the second-lowest total in modern playoff history.

Pippen led the Bulls' offense with 27 points on 11-of-14 shooting. "We realize they're a team that's banged up, and we just overpowered them," he said.

"We can't have pity on them," Jackson warned.

And they didn't. Especially not killer Mike, who scored 45 to close the series out in Game 4. The writers couldn't help but notice the irony.

He had worn uniform number 45 during his comeback the previous spring, until the Magic hounded him so much during the playoffs that he switched back to his old number 23.

Jordan assured the media that he had not run up his scoring just to make a point with the Magic. That's just how things worked out, he said.

Besides, the Bulls needed every bucket Jordan had to offer just to escape, 106-101.

The outcome wasn't retribution for last year's loss, Jackson insisted. But one thing was very clear. The Bulls were headed back to the Finals, the championship round.

"We have remained focused for the last four months to do one thing, and that's to win the championship," Rodman said. "It's not our goal – it's our destiny."

AFTER BATTLING ALL SEASON TO BE crowned NBA champions, the Chicago Bulls climbed close enough to see their glittering prize, only to discover they'd have to sit back a while and twiddle their thumbs.

The matter of winning their fourth title in six years turned into a tedious waiting game during late May and early June. The Bulls' sweep of Orlando in the Eastern Finals set up the problem. The Seattle SuperSonics had taken a 3-1 lead over the Utah Jazz in the Western Finals, only to watch the Jazz fight back and tie the series.

The result for the Bulls was a nine-day layoff waiting for Seattle to claim the seventh game, so at last the championship round finally could begin.

After all the sitting around, the 1996 NBA Finals opened on Wednesday, June 5, but even that didn't mean the Bulls' waiting was over. What lay ahead were several unexpected delays in Seattle.

The Bulls were 10-1 favorites to defeat the Sonics, despite Seattle's impressive 64 victories during the regular season, which meant that the Finals carried the anticipation of an unfolding coronation. As if that needed any further emphasis, England's Princess Di visited Chicago for a medical fundraiser as Game 1 was set to begin, leaving the city stuck with divided royalties.

Should the well-connected locals go the the Field Museum of Natural History for a candlelit evening of dinner and dancing with Her Royal Highness?

Or should they truck over to the United Center to watch the fallaway jumpers and slick reverses of His Royal Airness?

Even Deloris Jordan, Michael's mom and a serious Di fan, was confounded by the conflicting events. The Bulls or the ball? She decided to slip into an evening gown and catch dinner with the Princess, then change clothes and dash across town to watch Her Son Who Would Be King Again.

"I know Michael expects me to be there," she explained.

Others decided to break away from the ball for quick updates on radio and TV. Regardless, there were no extra seats at the United Center. The NBA had issued credentials to approximately 1,600 journalists from around the globe for the event.

The whole world would be watching, which had become standard procedure for just about all of Jordan's performances, particularly since the Bulls had added Rodman as a court jester. The team's resident rebounder did his part by showing up with a wildly spray-painted hairdo, a sort of graffiti in flames, with various red, green, blue hieroglyphics and symbols scrambled on his skull.

As usual, Rodman had made a major contribution to the off-court news of the day. An Idaho company announced it was marketing a Worm lollipop, a "bloated worm with Rodman's head on it," that sold for 99 cents in cherry, strawberry-banana, strawberry creme, root beer, grape and tutti-frutti flavors. And just recently, Rodman's lawyers had secured a court ban against a company distributing a T-shirt with a tattoo pattern remarkably similar to Rodman's own skin.

But if Rodman gave the championship proceedings an MTV feel, there were plenty of golden oldies on hand as a reminder of The Finals' 50-year tradition. In particular, Commissioner David Stern had invited hoary-faced Bill Russell, the ultimate pro basketball champion, as his guest. And new Charlotte coach Dave Cowens, himself an old Finals hand, stood courtside chatting up another championship series veteran, Maurice Lucas.

In fact, it was 20 years ago that Cowens and his Boston Celtics took on the upstart Phoenix Suns in a memorable Finals series, one that included a triple-overtime thriller.

THE NINE-DAY LAYOFF ALLOWED KUKOC'S BACK TO HEAL, AND HE RETURNED TO FORM WHEN THE SERIES STARTED.

THE BULLS KNEW THAT THE ANSWER TO ANOTHER TITLE WAS INTENSITY.

THE ACROBATIC WORM WAS EVERYWHERE.

Both the Sonics and Bulls held a place in that lore, the Bulls with their early '90s Threepeaters and the Sonics with back-to-back trips in 1978 and '79. Coached then by Lenny Wilkens, they had claimed the championship in 1979.

This latest edition from Seattle hoped to follow that tradition, and some observers thought they had the athletic talent and defensive pressure to turn back the Bulls.

Luc Longley, however, mostly approached the series with relief. After contending with Mourning, Ewing and Shaq in the Eastern play-offs, he no longer faced brute force in the low post. The Sonics started spindly Ervin Johnson at center, let him play a few minutes, then turned the game over to 6-9 veteran Sam Perkins, who got most of his offense from the perimeter.

As with every other Bulls' opponent, Seattle's big concern was holding back Jordan, who was asked by reporters if he could still launch the Air raids that made him famous.

"Can I still take off? I don't know," he said. "I haven't been able to try it because defenses don't guard me one-on-one anymore. But honestly, I probably can't do it. I like not knowing whether I can do it because that way, I still think I can. As long as I believe I can do something, that's all that matters."

As an added measure, Seattle coach George Karl had hired recently fired Toronto coach Brendan Malone to scout the Bulls during the playoffs. Malone, during his days as a Pistons assistant, had helped devise the infamous "Jordan Rules" to help defeat Chicago. The Sonics hoped that his perspective might help them find a deployment to slow down Jordan, who had averaged 32.1 points during the playoffs.

"You have to try to match their intensity," Malone advised. "Forget Xs and Os. They are going to try and cut your heart out right away, right from the first quarter."

Now, with Game 1 set to tip off, Malone stepped into the arena on his way to the Seattle bench and paused long enough to give Jackson a good-natured punch. Phil flinched and smiled.

The United Center crowd greeted the Sonics with a muffled, impolite boo that seemed to imply a lack of respect. In keeping with this mood, Rodman ignored Seattle forward Shawn Kemp as they brushed past each other heading toward center court for the opening tip.

The Sonics started the series with 6-10 Detlef Schrempf playing Jordan, but when Michael posted up, guard Hersey Hawkins went immediately to the double-team. Seldom one to force up a dumb shot, Jordan found Harper for an open three, and the 1996 Finals were off and running.

The surprise move by the Bulls was having Longley cover the athletic Kemp, who responded by dropping in a pair of early jumpers. Longley used his size to power in 12 first-half points with the Sonics obviously intent on forcing Jordan to pass. Pippen and Harper both found their offense, allowing Chicago to open an 11-point lead by the third quarter.

LONGLEY'S SIZE CREATED PROBLEMS FOR THE SONICS.

RODMAN HAD A CHAT WITH KARL.

The Sonics had seemed to drag a bit, the obvious aftereffects of their seven-game series with Utah, but they found their legs and pulled within 69-67 as the fourth quarter opened.

It was then that Kukoc regained his form. The layoff, he explained later, had given his back time to heal. Indeed, he scored 10 straight points in the first five minutes of the quarter. The outburst included a pair of treys. He was fouled on the second three-pointer and made the free throw, one of only three four-point plays in Finals history.

"I was waiting for just one good game to come," Kukoc said. "I thought I had to go out and post up some guys instead of hoping that my three-point shot would go in. So I did that, and after that happened, I took a couple of three-point shots, made them, and that opened up the game."

To go with Kukoc's scoring, the Bulls turned on their pressure, forcing seven turnovers in the fourth quarter alone, and won big, 107-90.

The Sonics were especially hurt by the loss to injury of big third guard

Nate McMillan, which left point guard Gary Payton shouldering most of the ballhandling duties alone.

Jordan topped the Bulls with 28 points, but Seattle's defensive effort had meant that his teammates got off to a good championship start. Pippen scored 21, Kukoc 18, Harper 15 and Longley 14.

Rodman finished with 13 rebounds and watched as the officials ejected Seattle reserve Frank Brickowski for a dubious attempt to engage him in a scuffle, a silly little ploy played out before the network cameras.

The circumstances left Karl furious. "Dennis Rodman is laughing at basketball," the Seattle coach said before Game 2. "It's silly to give him any credibility for what he does out there."

"A lot of people don't give me enough credit for being an adult," Rodman replied. "Yesterday was a perfect example that I can be under control."

In retrospect, Karl probably should have held back in provoking Rodman, because the Worm was

THE DEFENSE RENDERED THE SONIC BOOM A BUST.

SHAWN KEMP (40) WAS OUTSTANDING IN THE SERIES, BUT THE BULLS MADE HIM WORK FOR HIS POINTS.

ready with an answer in Game 2, a 20-rebound performance, including a record-tying 11 offensive rebounds that helped Chicago overcome 39 percent shooting.

Time and again, Rodman's rebounding allowed the Bulls to survive their all-too-frequent offensive lulls. Others played a role, as well. Although he struggled, Jordan willed

29 points into the hoop. And the defense forced another 20 Sonics turnovers, including a batch during a three-minute stretch of the third period, when Chicago pushed the margin from 66-64 to 76-65. Once again, it was Kukoc off the bench contributing the key offense. He hit two three-pointers. Then Pippen got a breakaway jam after a steal, which

was followed by a Kukoc slam on a pass from Jordan, whose anger had prompted the outburst in the first place.

"Are you scared?" he had asked Kukoc. "If you are, then sit down. If you're out here to shoot, then shoot."

Kukoc did, and the run provided enough margin for the Bulls to with-

stand a fourth-quarter Sonics surge. The Bulls opened an 81-68 lead, but fell into a stupor after Kukoc scored on a stickback with six minutes left. They would not get another field goal and were forced to hang on with free throws.

The Sonics pulled to 87-81, but missed on four straight possessions. In the last minute, they closed the

gap to 91-88, but Rodman got a rebound on a Kerr miss and later hit a big free throw after Pippen had missed a pair.

The Bulls knew they had escaped with a 92-88 victory but were happy to take whatever they could get. Harper, the key to their pressure defense, had reinjured his creaky knees, requiring that fluid be drawn

off one of them just before the game. That allowed him to play and contribute 12 points and the usual good defense, but it also meant that he would miss all or most of the next three games.

Karl found himself having to acknowledge just how important Rodman was to Chicago. "He's an amazing rebounder," the Sonics

AND RODMAN CONTINUED TO PROVIDE OFFENSE.

BUT JORDAN STILL CARRIED THE BULK OF THE LOAD.

coach said. "He was probably their MVP tonight."

With Harper's knee hurting, the Bulls figured they were in for a fight with the next three games in Seattle's Key Arena. But the Sonics were strangely subdued for Game 3. With Kukoc starting for the injured Harper, the Bulls were vulnerable defensively.

Yet Chicago forced the issue on offense from the opening tip. With

Jordan scoring 12 points, the Bulls leaped to a 34-12 lead by the end of the first quarter. For all intents and purposes, the game was over.

By halftime, Chicago had stretched the lead to 62-38, and although Seattle pulled within a dozen twice in the third, the margin was just too large to overcome. The second half was marked by Rodman's smirking antics that once again brought the Sonics' frustrations to

the boiling point. Brickowski was ejected for a flagrant foul with six minutes left, and the Key Arena fans, so rowdy in earlier rounds of the playoffs, witnessed the display in numbed silence.

Jordan finished with 36, but the big surprise was 19 from Longley, who had struggled in Game 2. Asked what had turned the big center's game around, Jackson replied, "Verbal bashing by everybody on the club. I don't think anybody's ever been attacked by as many people as Luc after Friday's game. Tex gave him an earful, and Michael did, too. I tried the last few days to build his confidence back up."

Apparently the treatment worked, because Longley's size was one of several elements of the Bulls attack that troubled the Sonics. Both Pippen and Kukoc responded with solid floor games. Pippen had 12 points, nine assists and eight rebounds, while Kukoc finished with 14 points, seven rebounds and seven assists.

With the victory, the Bulls were up 3-0, on the verge of a sweep that would give them a 15-1 run through the playoffs, the most successful postseason record in NBA history.

With Game 4 set for Wednesday, the next two days of practice took on the air of a coronation, with the media hustling to find comparisons between the Bulls and pro basketball's other great teams from the past.

ESPN analyst Jack Ramsay, who had coached the '77 Trail Blazers to an NBA title and served as general manager of Philadelphia's great 1967 team, said the Bulls just might be the greatest defensive team of all time. "The best defenders in the game are Pippen and Jordan..." he said. "They're just so tough. In each playoff series, they take away one more thing from the opponent, and then you're left standing out there naked, without a stitch of clothes. It's embarrassing."

The key to the Bulls' drive was Jordan, Ramsay added. "He is such a fierce competitor that he brings everybody beyond their individual levels. I watched Steve Kerr, who had the reputation of being a no-defense guy, a good spot-up shooter. Now you watch him, he's out there playing defense, challenging everybody that he plays, he's right in their face. He may get beaten, but he's not going to back down from the chore. He now puts the ball on the floor and creates his own shot. That's something he never did before.

DESPITE PIPPEN'S STRANGE GYRATIONS, THINGS WENT WELL IN GAME 3 AS LONGLEY AND KERR SCORED INSIDE AND OUT.

BUT WITH HARPER INJURED, THE BULLS DEFENSE HAD NO PRESSURE. THE SONICS GAINED CONFIDENCE AND PULLED THE SERIES TO 3-2.

Michael's influence on all those players is tremendous," he said.

"They play as a team, and there appears to be no selfishness. There's no evidence of ego. The guys from the bench, they go in the game, and when they come out, you don't see any of them look up at the clock and look at the coach. They go over and sit down. When they come in, the guys on the floor bring them right into the game and get shots for them. They all know their roles, and they all can fill their roles."

Arriving for the interview session Tuesday just as the Bulls were leaving, the Sonics' Kemp wasted little time blasting his team for giving up in Game 3. Any member of the team who failed to show up for Game 4 would be a coward, Kemp said.

The reporters gathered around him listened politely and took notes. But it seemed pretty clear that the series was over.

Tex Winter was worried that the Bulls were being seduced by all the talk about the greatest team ever, and later he would kick himself for not complaining louder about it. But it wasn't just the talk that did them in.

Ron Harper had been unable to practice for more than a week, and his availability for Game 4 was in doubt. The Sonics, on the other hand, were optimistic that Nate McMillan would be able to go.

Three hours before game time, NBA officials gathered in Key Arena to practice the awards ceremony in the event that the Bulls won. This was standard procedure, but the Sonics players arrived during the practice, and it added to the sting.

In their locker room, the Bulls tried to put off the nervousness. Jordan, his blue suit jacket removed, perched in the corner, intently filling out ticket voucher envelopes. In the opposite corner, Rodman sat in his usual pajamas turned inside-out, his headphones half-mast, doing his best to ignore the furtive questions of NBC reporter Jim Gray. Stretched out on the floor a few feet away, a shirtless Scottie Pippen screwed his focus on a video replay of Game 3, trying to ignore the two international TV crews that hovered over him.

Finally, 45 minutes before game time, the media were ushered out of the locker room, where the Bulls remained sequestered even through the national anthem.

Harry Connick Jr. opened the game by singing what was perhaps the most restrained rendition in Finals history. He implored the Key Arena crowd to sing along with him, but the best the gathering of 17,000 could produce was a light murmur. If the Sonics played the same way, the Bulls seemed set to win their fourth.

Harper had vowed he would be able to play, and sure enough, he was in the starting lineup. But his knees allowed him no more than token minutes, which left a huge gap in the Bulls' pressure. It took the Sonics a few minutes to discover this. They missed their first four shots, but a Kemp slam at 9:26 finally pulled the crowd all the way out of bed. The Sonics felt a glimmer of confidence. Midway through the period, they got their first home lead of the series and never looked back.

The outcome was really settled by a second-quarter blitz from which Chicago never recovered. Actually, the burst of momentum began with 1:28 left in the first when McMillan appeared, and the arena crowd pounded out a prolonged thunder, bringing to mind New York Knicks center Willis Reed's limping appearance in the 1970 Finals against Los Angeles.

When McMillan dished Payton an assist for a 25-19 Seattle lead, the building thundered again, touching off a run that would take the Sonics to a 36-21 lead. Kukoc scored to stop the flow, but then the Sonics zoomed off again while the Bulls racked up misses and turnovers. On the bench, Winter scribbled furiously trying to keep up with the mistakes on his chart.

In a series sorely lacking in drama, the Bulls finally had managed to

produce some – falling behind by 21 points. They had covered worse spreads during the regular season, so the circumstances begged the question: Could they come back?

In a word, no.

Against Orlando, when the Bulls had fallen behind by 18, Jackson had quipped in the locker room at the half that "we got 'em where we want 'em." There was none of that this time.

The Bulls pushed as Jordan furiously berated both his teammates and the officials, but without Harper, the defense offered no real pressure, because there was no one to free Jordan and Pippen to do their damage.

With four minutes left in the period, the arena operators played a scoreboard look-alike game during a time-out, flashing first a photo of Madonna, then Rodman in drag with his feather boa. The arena roared in delight as the PA system blared the Aerosmith classic "Dude Looks Like A Lady."

The fourth period offered more of the same, which Jackson witnessed morosely, chin in palm. Midway through the quarter, Jordan was called for a double dribble. Furious, he stomped his foot, obviously rattled.

He left the game minutes later, having hit just six of 19, barked furiously from the bench in the closing minutes, with Pippen laughing, squeezing his shoulder. Easy, Mike. We'll get 'em in the next one.

That, for sure, was their intent. At the next day's practice, Jackson was asked if he feared that the Sonics had gotten their confidence. No, he replied, at this level it was a matter of more than confidence.

Funny, but it sure seemed that way in Game 5.

Once again, Harper was unable to go, which put Kukoc into the lineup. Pippen came out before the opening tip, stuck his fist in Luc's chest and whacked him three quick times. Time to come around, big fella.

The Bulls struggled to play well, but again there was no teeth in their

URGED ON BY HIS TEAMMATES, LONGLEY AGAIN PLAYED LARGE.

HARPER SHOOK OFF THE PAIN AND PLAYED 38 BIG MINUTES IN GAME 6.

JORDAN AND RODMAN RESUMED CONTROL OF THE BOARDS.

defense. The Sonics had only two unforced turnovers at halftime.

Still, the game stayed tight. The Bulls trailed 62-60 at the end of the third and hung around early in the fourth. With eight minutes to go, Pippen put home a Randy Brown miss to pull Chicago within 71-69, but the Sonics answered with an 11-0 run that the Bulls couldn't answer.

With their heroes up 80-69, the Sonics crowd pushed the decibel level above 117. On the floor, a fan held up a sign that said, "Dennis' Departure Will Leave Us Sleazeless in Seattle."

Pippen and Kerr hit treys that made it 84-77 with two minutes to go, but the effort took them no further. Rodman showed his anger when Jackson replaced him with Brown; Haley tried to calm him, but Rodman knocked his hand away. Jordan and Pippen, too, had shown flashes of anger, and the media that had been ready to crown them just two days earlier began noting that the Bulls seemed fragmented and tired.

Finally, it ended 89-78, and for the second straight game, the arena air glittered with golden confetti.

POISED TO WIN A CHAMPIONSHIP, JORDAN STEPPED TO CENTER STAGE.

The series, miraculously, was returning to Chicago. "The Joy of Six," the Seattle newspapers declared the next day in a headline.

The Bulls had shot 37 percent from the floor and only 3 for 26 from three-point land, 11.5 percent.

"It's all on them now," Payton said.

They kept their game faces at Saturday's practice, but the Bulls admitted later that they were rattled. Now, however, they were back home, with a 3-2 series lead. The Sonics faced the task of winning in the United Center, not once, but twice.

So much hinged on whether Harper could play. In the locker room before the game, he vowed he would. He had never taken so much as an anti-inflammatory, saying he didn't believe in putting drugs of any kind in his body. But he said he would play with pain. And that was all his teammates needed to know.

Game 6 was played on Father's Day, June 16th, and Jordan felt the rush of emotion, much of it stemming from thoughts of James Jordan, not only his dad but friend and advisor. "He's always on my mind," Jordan said.

Michael decided to dedicate the game to his father's memory. Would it be too much to handle? Even Jordan didn't know that answer.

For the third straight time, league officials had spent the pregame hours practicing the trophy presentation. Would they finally get it right?

Once again the Bulls stayed in the locker room during the anthem, but no sooner had Jesse Campbell started singing than the United Center crowd launched into a roar. Across the arena they were calling for the Bulls, calling for their team to come out and end this matter. The roar during player introductions was deafening, and happily for the Bulls, one of the starters who trotted out into the bedlam was Ron Harper.

At tipoff, the audience sent forth another blast of noise, just in case the Bulls didn't get the message the first time. Then yet another explosion followed moments later when

MICHAEL WAS FINALS MVP FOR A FOURTH TIME.

THE JORDAN CHILDREN SEND THEIR WISHES TO DAD ON FATHERS DAY.

IT WAS FINALLY SAFE TO START CELEBRATING.

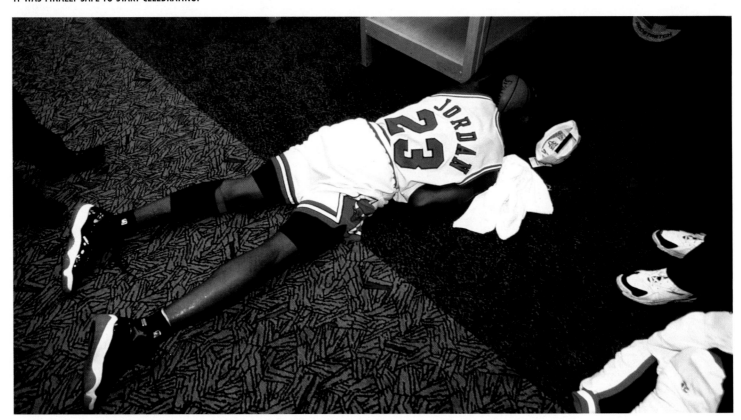

OVERCOME WITH EMOTION, JORDAN TRIED TO ESCAPE THE CAMERAS BUT COLLAPSED ON THE TRAINING ROOM FLOOR.

Pippen went to the hoop with a sweet underhand scoop to open the scoring. The building would rock throughout the game, with the decibel level topping 100, just like in old Chicago Stadium. The crowd was not going to allow the Bulls to lose.

With Harper back, the Bulls' pressure returned, and they picked the Sonics clean time and again. On this momentous occasion, Harper would play 38 minutes, and when he paused, an assistant trainer coated his knee with a spray anesthetic.

Spurred on by Harper's presence, Pippen pushed the Bulls out of the gate in the first period with seven points and two steals, giving Chicago a 16-12 lead.

The Bulls used more of the same to extend the lead in the second, as Jackson leaned back in his seat with his arms folded. Fifty feet away, Karl strolled the baseline, downcast, his hands jammed in his pockets. The lead moved to 27-18 on another Pippen steal and dish to Jordan, but the Sonics pushed right back, moving to 31-27 on Kemp's jam.

Another run by the Bulls punched it back up to 41-29, then Seattle answered again, pulling within 45-38 at the half.

The Bulls, though, saved their killer run for the third, a 19-9 spurt capped by Pippen dishing to Rodman on the break, with the Worm flipping in a little reverse shot and ramming his fists skyward, bringing yet another outburst from the building, which got louder yet when Rodman made the free throw for a 62-47 lead.

Just when it seemed they would be run out of the building, the Sonics responded with a 9-0 burst. To turn Seattle back, Kerr launched a long three over Perkins, and the Bulls ended the third up nine, 67-58.

Jackson had left Jordan on the bench for a long stretch at the end of the third, so that Michael would be fresh for the finish. But with Jordan facing double-teams and his own rush of emotions, at least some of the momentum had to come from

Kukoc, who canned a three from the corner to push it to 70-58.

Later, Kukoc knocked down another trey, for a 75-61 lead. Rodman, meanwhile, was on his way to grabbing 19 rebounds, including another 11 on the offensive board to tie the record that he had just equalled in Game 2. Then Luc tried to slam, drew Kemp's sixth foul, and made two free throws to jack the score to 79-65.

Pippen followed that with a deep trey, and the party atmosphere rum-

bled. Kerr hit a jumper to drive it to 84-68 at 2:44, and the whole building was dancing to "Whoop, There It Is!"

Yes, there it was, in game number 100, the sweet conclusion to this Great Bull Run, with the Luvabulls wiggling during a timeout, the building hopping, the scoreboard flashing. In the middle of this delirium, the standing ovations came one after another. The dagger, Pippen's final trey on a kick-out from Jordan, came at 57 seconds.

THEIR FACES SAID IT ALL.

Moments later, on the last possession of this magical season, Jordan dribbled near midcourt, then relinquished the ball to Pippen for one last delirious heave.

As soon as it was over, Jackson stepped out to hug Pippen and Jordan, who broke lose to grab the game ball and tumble to the floor with Randy Brown. Pippen gave Kukoc a big squeeze, then grabbed Harper, his old buddy, to tell him,

"Believe it! Dreams really do come true."

Even the suits on the bench, Jack Haley and Jason Caffey, exchanged chest bumps, and Kerr and Buechler, the Arizona teammates, embraced over the conclusion to their wonderful, improbable journey.

Nearby, Jackson shared a quiet hug with Dennis, Dennis nodding, Dennis at peace, and Luc there taking it all in with a big Aussie grin.

Then Jordan was gone, the game ball clutched behind his head, disappearing into the locker room, trying to escape those damn NBC cameras, searching for haven in the trainer's room, weeping on the floor in joy and pain, feeling the greatness and the sadness of it all.

"I'm sorry I was away for 18 months," Michael would say later after being named Finals MVP. "I'm happy I'm back, and I'm happy to bring a championship back to Chicago."

Back in the arena, the two Jerrys, Reinsdorf and Krause, beamed in the thrill of the moment, anticipating David Stern's presentation of the trophy. In a nod to 1992, the last time the Bulls won a championship at home, the players jumped up on the courtside press table for a victory jig to acknowledge the fans. Right with them was Rodman, already shirtless, living the vision just as he knew it would be.

"I think we can consider ourselves the greatest team of all time," Pippen said with satisfaction.

Strangely, it was Karl who put the whole show in perspective. "This

Bulls team is like the Pistons or Celtics, or some team from the '80s," he said. "This is the '90s, but they play with a learned mentality from an earlier time. This is an old-time package.

"I don't know about the Bird Era or the Magic Era. They were great teams, but this Bulls team has that same basic mentality. I like their heart and I like their philosophy."

Which had Jordan already gazing into the future. "Five is the next number," he said with that world-famous smile.

Yes, perhaps, but this was one for the grandkids. "There was this team," you'll tell them, "and there was this player..."

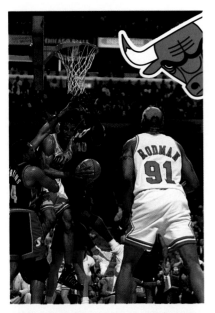

Regular Season Statistics 1995-96

Date	Opponent	Team/Opp Total		High Scoring	High Rebounds	High Assists	Atten.
3-Nov	Charlotte	W105-91	1–0	Jordan-42	Rodman-11	Jordan-7	23,862
4-Nov	Boston	W107-85	2–0	Pippen-21	Longley-8/Rodman-8	Kukoc-5/Pippen-5	23,608
7-Nov	Toronto	W117-108	3–0	Jordan-38	Rodman-13	Pippen-8	23,102
9-Nov	at Cleveland	W106-88	4–0	Jordan-29	Pippen-13	Pippen-12	20,562
11-Nov	Portland	W110-106	5–0	Jordan-36	Pippen-9	Jordan-7	23,384
14-Nov	at Orlando	L88-94	5–1	Jordan-23	Pippen-10	Jordan-6/Pippen-6	17,248
15-Nov	Cleveland	W113-94	6–1	Pippen-27	Caffey-8	Pippen-8	23,257
17-Nov	New Jersey	W109-94	7–1	Kukoc-19	Longley-8	Kukoc-7	23,312
21-Nov	at Dallas	W108-102(OT)	8–1	Jordan-36	Pippen-12	Pippen-7	17,502
22-Nov	at San Antonio	W103-94	9–1	Jordan-38	Longley-11	Pippen-13	35,888
24-Nov	at Utah	W90-85	10–1	Jordan-34	Longley-10	Jordan-6	19,911
26-Nov	at Seattle	L92-97	10–2	Jordan-22	Pippen-12	Pippen-5	17,072
27-Nov	at Portland	W107-104	11–2	Jordan-33	Wennington-5/Pippen-5	Pippen-10	21,401
30-Nov	at Vancouver	W94-88	12–2	Jordan-29	Longley-10	Pippen-8	19,193
2-Dec	at L.A.-Clippers	W104-98	13–2	Jordan-37	Pippen-13	Pippen-6	18,321
6-Dec	New York	W101-94	14–2	Jordan-22/Pippen-22	Rodman-20	Jordan-8/Pippen-8	23,828
8-Dec	San Antonio	W106-87	15–2	Jordan-28	Rodman-21	Jordan-6	23,802
9-Dec	at Milwaukee	W118-106	16–2	Jordan-45	Rodman-21	Pippen-6	18,633
13-Dec	Orlando	W112-103	17–2	Jordan-36	Rodman-19	Pippen-6	23,895
14-Dec	at Atlanta	W127-108	18–2	Pippen-30	Rodman-10	Kukoc-8/Pippen-8	16,378
16-Dec	L.A. Lakers	W108-88	19–2	Pippen-33	Rodman-15	Jordan-6/Pippen-6	23,824
18-Dec	at Boston	W123-114	20–2	Jordan-37/Pippen-37	Rodman-17	Pippen-12	18,624
19-Dec	Dallas	W114-101	21–2	Jordan-32	Rodman-13	Kerr-6	23,208
22-Dec	Toronto	W113-104	22–2	Jordan-27	Jordan-10	Jordan-5	22,987
23-Dec	Utah	W100-86	23–2	Jordan-30	Rodman-12	Jordan-8	23,906
26-Dec	at Indiana	L97-103	23–3	Jordan-30	Rodman-11	Pippen-6	16,728
29-Dec	Indiana	W120-93	24–3	Jordan-29	Rodman-16	Pippen-8	23,739
30-Dec	Atlanta	W95-93	25–3	Jordan-33	Rodman-21	Jordan-6	23,587
3-Jan	Houston	W100-86	26–3	Jordan-38	Rodman-15	Pippen-9	23,854
4-Jan	at Charlotte	W117-93	27–3	Jordan-27	Rodman-11	Harper-7	24,042
6-Jan	Milwaukee	W113-84	28–3	Jordan-32	Rodman-16	Pippen-6	23,801
10-Jan	Seattle	W113-87	29–3	Jordan-35	Jordan-14	Jordan-5/Longley-5/Pippen-5	23,877
13-Jan	at Philadelphia	W120-93	30–3	Jordan-48	Rodman-16	Pippen-10	18,168
15-Jan	at Washington	W116-109	31–3	Jordan-46	Rodman-15	Pippen-6	18,756
16-Jan	Philadelphia	W116-104	32–3	Jordan-32	Rodman-21	Rodman-10	23,587
18-Jan	at Toronto	W92-89	33–3	Jordan-38	Rodman-13	Pippen-4/Rodman-4	36,118
21-Jan	at Detroit	W111-96	34–3	Jordan-36	Rodman-9	Pippen-6	21,454
23-Jan	at New York	W99-79	35–3	Jordan-33	Rodman-13	Pippen-6	19,763
24-Jan	Vancouver	W104-84	36–3	Pippen-30	Rodman-16	Harper-7	23,652
26-Jan	Miami	W102-80	37–3	Jordan-25	Rodman-16	Pippen-5/Rodman-5	23,814
28-Jan	Phoenix	W93-82	38–3	Jordan-31	Rodman-20	Jordan-6	23,927
30-Jan	at Houston	W98-87	39–3	Pippen-28	Pippen-12	Pippen-5	16,285
1-Feb	at Sacramento	W105-85	40–3	Jordan-27	Rodman-21	Kukoc-5	17,317
2-Feb	at L.A. Lakers	W99-84	41–3	Pippen-30	Rodman-23	Jordan-7	17,505
4-Feb	at Denver	L99-105	41–4	Jordan-39	Rodman-12	Harper-5/Pippen-5/Wennington-5	17,171
6-Feb	at Phoenix	L96-106	41–5	Jordan-28	Rodman-14	Pippen-8	19,023
7-Feb	at Golden State	W99-95	42–5	Jordan-40	Rodman-18	Jordan-6	15,025
13-Feb	Washington	W111-98	43–5	Jordan-32	Rodman-16	Pippen-4	23,494
15-Feb	at Detroit	W112-109(OT)	44–5	Jordan-32	Rodman-19	Pippen-6	21,454
16-Feb	at Minnesota	W103-100	45–5	Jordan-35	Rodman-19	Pippen-7	20,214
18-Feb	at Indiana	W110-102	46–5	Jordan-44	Rodman-23	Jordan-7	16,770
20-Feb	Cleveland	W102-76	47–5	Harper-22	Rodman-15	Pippen-8	23,604
22-Feb	at Atlanta	W96-91	48–5	Jordan-34	Rodman-20	Pippen-10	16,378
23-Feb	at Miami	L104-113	48–6	Jordan-31	Rodman-11	Pippen-6	15,200
25-Feb	Orlando	W111-91	49–6	Kukoc-24	Rodman-17	Jordan-7	24,102
27-Feb	Minnesota	W120-99	50–6	Jordan-35	Rodman-24	Jordan-7	23,716
1-Mar	Golden State	W110-87	51–6	Pippen-25	Rodman-17	Jordan-6	23,596
2-Mar	Boston	W107-75	52–6	Jordan-21	Rodman-15	Jordan-8	23,721
5-Mar	Milwaukee	W115-106	53–6	Jordan-33	Rodman-9	Harper-7/Kukoc-7	23,547
7-Mar	Detroit	W102-81	54–6	Jordan-53	Rodman-13	Pippen-10	23,369
10-Mar	at New York	L72-104	54–7	Jordan-32	Rodman-10	Pippen-5	19,763
13-Mar	Washington	W103-86	55–7	Jordan-37	Rodman-14	Jordan-5	23,652
15-Mar	Denver	W108-87	56–7	Jordan-33	Rodman-15	Kukoc-10	23,692
16-Mar	at New Jersey	W97-93	57–7	Jordan-37	Jordan-16	Jordan-5	20,049
18-Mar	at Philadelphia	W98-94	58–7	Jordan-38	Jordan-11	Kukoc-11	18,168
19-Mar	Sacramento*	W89-67	59–7	Jordan-20	Jordan-9	Kukoc-7	23,312
21-Mar	New York	W107-86	60–7	Jordan-36	Jordan-11	Kukoc-5/Jordan-5	23,802
24-Mar	at Toronto	L108-109	60–8	Jordan-36	Jordan-9/Kukoc-9/Pippen-9	Pippen-8	36,131
28-Mar	Atlanta	W111-80	61–8	Kukoc-24	Pippen-11	Pippen-8	23,642
30-Mar	L.A. Clippers	W106-85	62–8	Pippen-22	Jordan-9/Kukoc-9	Jordan-6	23,764
2-Apr	at Miami	W110-92	63–8	Jordan-32/Pippen-32	Rodman-13	Harper-8	15,200
4-Apr	Miami**	W100-92	64–8	Jordan-40	Rodman-12	Pippen-8	23,702
5-Apr	at Charlotte	W126-92	65–8	Pippen-28	Rodman-17	Pippen-14	24,042
7-Apr	at Orlando	W90-86	66–8	Jordan-27	Pippen-13/Rodman-13	Harper-5/Pippen-5	17,248
8-Apr	Charlotte	L97-98	66–9	Jordan-40	Rodman-17	Pippen-6	23,590
11-Apr	at New Jersey#	W113-100	67–9	Jordan-17	Rodman-12	Kukoc-6	20,049
12-Apr	Philadelphia	W112-82	68–9	Jordan-23	Rodman-16	Pippen-6	23,633
14-Apr	at Cleveland	W98-72	69–9	Jordan-32	Jordan-12	Kukoc-5	20,562
16-Apr	at Milwaukee	W86-80	70–9	Jordan-22	Rodman-19	Jordan-4/Kukoc-4/Rodman-4	18,633
18-Apr	Detroit	W110-79	71–9	Jordan-30	Rodman-18	Pippen-8	23,614
20-Apr	Indiana	L99-100	71–10	Jordan-24	Rodman-15	Brown-6/Jordan-6	23,784
21-Apr	at Washington	W103-93	72–10	Jordan-26	Rodman-11	Pippen-5	18,756

*–Bulls clinch Central Division Championship and a playoff berth.
**–Bulls clinch home court advantage in playoffs for the Eastern Conference.
#–Bulls clinch home court advantage throughout playoffs.

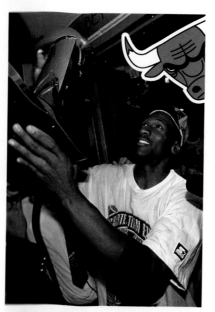

Regular Season Player Statistics 1995-96

Player	G	GS	FIELD GOALS MIN	FG	FGA	PCT	3-POINT FG FG	FGA	PCT	FREE THROWS FT	FTA	PCT	REBOUNDS OFF	DEF	TOT	AST	PTS	AVG
Jordan	82	82	3090	916	1850	.495	111	260	.427	548	657	.834	148	395	543	352	2491	30.4
Pippen	77	77	2825	563	1216	.463	150	401	.374	220	324	.679	152	344	496	452	1496	19.4
Kukoc	81	20	2103	386	787	.490	87	216	.403	206	267	.772	115	208	323	287	1065	13.1
Longley	62	62	1641	242	502	.482	0	0	—	80	103	.777	104	214	318	119	564	9.1
Kerr	82	0	1919	244	482	.506	122	237	.515	78	84	.929	25	85	110	192	688	8.4
Harper	80	80	1886	234	501	.467	28	104	.269	98	139	.705	74	139	213	208	594	7.4
Rodman	64	57	2088	146	304	.480	3	27	.111	56	106	.528	356	596	952	160	351	5.5
Wennington	71	20	1065	169	343	.493	1	1	1.000	37	43	.860	58	116	174	46	376	5.3
Haley	1	0	7	2	6	.333	0	0	—	1	2	.500	1	1	2	0	5	5
Salley (TOT)	42	6	673	63	140	.450	0	0	—	59	85	.694	46	94	140	54	185	4.4
Salley (CHI)	17	0	191	12	35	.343	0	0	—	12	20	.600	20	23	43	15	36	2.1
Buechler	74	0	740	112	242	.463	40	90	.444	14	22	.636	45	66	111	56	278	3.8
Simpkins	60	12	685	77	160	.481	1	1	1.000	61	97	.629	66	90	156	38	216	3.6
Edwards	28	0	274	41	110	.373	0	0	—	16	26	.615	15	25	40	11	98	3.5
Caffey	57	0	545	71	162	.438	1	0	.000	40	68	.588	51	60	111	24	182	3.2
Brown	68	0	671	78	192	.406	1	11	.091	28	46	.609	17	49	66	73	185	2.7
BULLS	82	—	19730	3293	6892	.478	544	1349	.403	1495	2004	.746	1247	2411	3658	2033	8625	105.2
OPPONENTS	82	—	19730	2880	6428	.448	437	1249	.350	1424	1985	.717	981	2136	3117	1592	7621	92.9

Team Statistics by Game for 1996 Playoffs

Date	Opponent	Team/Opp	Total	High Scoring	High Rebounds	High Assists	Atten.
26-Apr	**Miami**	W102-85	1–0	Jordan-35	Rodman-10	Kerr-3/Kukoc-3/Pippen-3	24,104
28-Apr	**Miami**	W106-75	2–0	Jordan-29	Pippen-8	Pippen-8	24,202
1-May	at Miami	W112-91	3–0	Jordan-26	Pippen-18	Pippen-10	15,200
5-May	**New York**	W91-84	4–0	Jordan-44	Rodman-12	Pippen-7	24,394
7-May	**New York**	W91-80	5–0	Jordan-28	Rodman-19	Pippen-6	24,328
11-May	at New York	L99-102(OT)	5–1	Jordan-46	Rodman-16	Pippen-6	19,763
12-May	at New York	W94-91	6–1	Jordan-27	Rodman-19	Jordan-8	19,763
14-May	**New York**	W94-81	7–1	Jordan-35	Rodman-12	Harper-5/Jordan-5	24,396
19-May	**Orlando**	W121-83	8–1	Jordan-21	Rodman-21	Kukoc-10	24,411
21-May	**Orlando**	W93-88	9–1	Jordan-35	Rodman-12	Pippen-9	24,395
25-May	at Orlando	W86-67	10–1	Pippen-27	Rodman-16	Pippen-7	17,248
27-May	at Orlando	W106-101	11–1	Jordan-45	Rodman-14	Pippen-8	17,248
5-Jun	**Seattle**	W107-90	12–1	Jordan-28	Rodman-13	Harper-7	24,544
7-Jun	**Seattle**	W92-88	13–1	Jordan-29	Rodman-20	Jordan-8	24,544
9-Jun	at Seattle	W108-86	14–1	Jordan-36	Rodman-10	Pippen-9	17,072
12-Jun	at Seattle	L86-107	14–2	Jordan-23	Rodman-14	Pippen-8	17,072
14-Jun	at Seattle	L78-89	14–3	Jordan-26	Rodman-12	Pippen-5	17,072
16-Jun	**Seattle**	W87-75	15–3	Jordan-22	Rodman-19	Jordan-7	24,544

1996 Playoffs Player Statistics/All Rounds Combined

Player	G	GS	FIELD GOALS MIN	FG	FGA	PCT	3-POINT FG FG	FGA	PCT	FREE THROWS FT	FTA	PCT	REBOUNDS OFF	DEF	TOT	AST	PTS	AVG
Jordan	18	18	733	187	407	.459	25	62	.403	153	187	.818	31	58	89	74	552	30.7
Pippen	18	18	742	112	287	.390	30	105	.286	51	80	.638	62	91	153	107	305	16.9
Kukoc	15	5	439	59	151	.391	13	68	.191	31	37	.838	19	44	63	58	162	10.8
Harper	18	16	494	57	134	.425	15	47	.319	29	42	.690	26	41	67	45	158	8.8
Longley	18	18	439	61	130	.469	0	0	—	28	37	.757	34	48	82	28	150	8.3
Rodman	18	15	620	50	103	.485	0	0	—	35	59	.593	98	149	247	37	135	7.5
Kerr	18	0	357	39	87	.448	17	53	.321	27	31	.871	3	15	18	31	122	6.8
Wennington	18	0	169	26	50	.520	0	1	.000	2	4	.500	11	19	30	9	54	3
Brown	16	0	112	16	28	.571	3	6	.500	9	12	.750	3	7	10	7	44	2.8
Buechler	17	0	127	18	38	.474	8	21	.381	2	4	.500	2	8	10	6	46	2.7
Edwards	6	0	28	4	9	.444	0	0	—	3	4	.750	0	4	4	0	11	1.8
Salley	16	0	85	6	11	.545	0	0	—	2	7	.286	4	7	11	6	14	0.9
TEAM	18	—	4345	635	1435	.443	111	363	.306	372	504	.738	293	491	784	408	1753	97.4
OPPONENTS	18	—	4345	565	1274	.443	93	323	.288	340	470	.723	185	457	642	289	1563	86.8

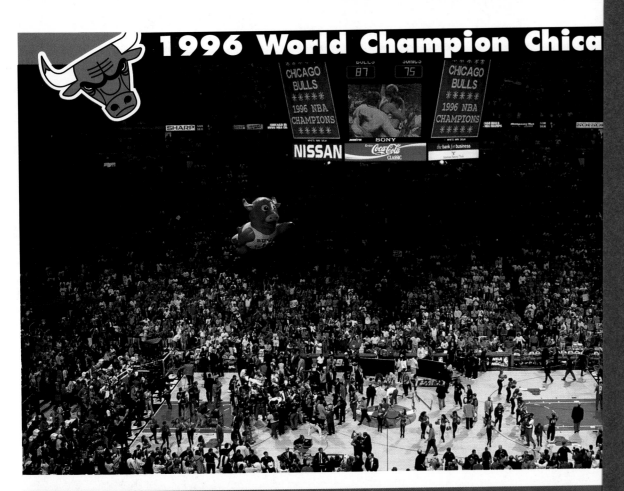

Back Row L to R: Toni Kukoc, Jud Buechler, Jason Caffey, James Edwards, Bill Wennington, Dickey Simpkins, Jack Haley, Randy Brown
Front Row L to R: Luc Longley, Dennis Rodman, Michael Jordan, Scottie Pippen, Ron Harper, Steve Kerr